BY GUESS AND BY GOD

BY GUESS AND BY GOD

THE STORY OF THE BRITISH SUBMARINES IN THE WAR

BY WILLIAM GUY CARR

WITH A PREFACE BY ADMIRAL S. S. HALL

ILLUSTRATED FROM PHOTOGRAPHS

FIRST EDITION 1930

REPRINT EDITION 2016

dauphin publications

TO MY WIFE

Admiral Hall, who has written the following preface, commanded the British Submarine Service for the greater period of the war. He was the directing power and he conceived many of the ideas which caused drastic changes to be made in the size and character of British submarines.

PREFACE

For the period of the Great War and for some years thereafter the very word "submarine" was repugnant to us; the terrible indignities that we suffered by reason of these parvenus could not easily be forgotten. The situation to those who had not seen it was exasperating.

Think of it! With the largest armada the world has ever seen at anchor in Scapa, with an auxiliary patrol of some four thousand vessels specially equipped for anti-submarine patrols, and with the assistance of the whole world's navies, excepting those of Germany and Austria, we steadily lost on an average one hundred and thirty vessels per month from enemy submarine action. In the active period of submarine warfare the average sinkings were six per diem. What wonder the exploits of

our submarine service were to a great extent lost
sight of in the general feeling of impatience and
bewilderment with which we looked upon the
whole matter.

Our traditional naval conduct was of no avail.
We went about feeling as though we were being
kicked in the back without being able to retaliate.
For this reason, Lieutenant Carr's book will be
welcomed as doing justice to a service that richly
deserves it, and particularly to the commanding
officers he mentions by name and upon whom fell
the duty of establishing a tradition for a new service.

The book comes at a time when such questions
as the limitation, humanitation, and even the abolition of submarines are more in the public eye
than the glorification of war deeds, and although
those who look for any guidance on these matters
will not find them on the surface, they will find
them if they look a little deeper.

They will notice that the stirring events which
Carr describes invariably assume an intimate personal relation with the character and ability of the
commanding officer, and herein lies the crux of the
whole matter of humanity and limitation of the
size of submarines.

I leave aside the question of abolition, for when
this was first mooted I happened to be in contact

PREFACE

with some French submarine officers at Toulon where the subject was treated with great hilarity.

Britain is a great naval power because she is a widely spread empire dependent upon sea communications. These communications have still to be safeguarded by surface vessels. We know and everyone knows that if any future enemy possesses a flotilla of submarines, however small, the endurance of our fleet will be cut down by at least fifty per cent because its ships will have to proceed always at a high speed on a zig-zag course, protected by large numbers of destroyers. This produces such a restrictive influence on all our sea operations that it is little wonder we desire the abolition of submarines, but to expect other nations not so affected to agree is, as I have said, nothing less than ludicrous.

Apart from abolition, however, this book will help to emphasize the overwhelming importance in submarine matters of the character and abilities of those who command them.

In surface vessels there are several factors which may bring success—in spite of the commanding officer. A ship may be a good shooting ship; an excellent chief of staff, mistakes on the part of the enemy, assistance from other vessels are some of these factors. In submarines none of these count. One man only, the commanding officer, can see, and he only with one eye. No one can help him. Germany had some four hundred submarine captains during the war but over sixty per cent of the damage they did was acomplished by but twenty-two of these four hundred officers. The inference is obvious. The one and great difficulty in submarine warfare is to find a sufficiency of officers such as the writer portrays, officers who will rise superior to the incidental intricacies of these complicated vessels, who will make their opportunities and take advantage of them when found under conditions of hardship and acute discomfort.

Fortunately, not every nation can produce such men, and if they cannot we can safely let them have as many and as large submarines as they like. This book will, I believe, make this quite clear to the discriminating reader.

S. S. HALL,
Admiral.

"The Shelters," Hamble,
March, 1930.

ILLUSTRATIONS

AN INTRODUCTORY NOTE

Two explanations are necessary.

"BY GUESS AND BY GOD" *was a phrase coined during the war by navigating officers of British submarines to describe the manner of their navigating. A surface ship in peace time proceeding on her way without celestial or other aids to navigation goes "by dead reckoning." A submarine in war time, with all artificial aids to navigation removed, with no chance to take a sight for days on end, harassed by the enemy, with compasses often acting queerly, went "by guess and by God." Blind as bats, we guessed and prayed inwardly that we guessed right: the rest was in the hands of Providence.*

Throughout this book, the Submarine Service is referred to as "the Trade." Before the war a term of opprobrium coined by the pukka navy to describe officers who looked more like plumbers' assistants while on duty than spic-and-span naval officers, the name took on a different significance during the war, and was accepted throughout the under-water branch of the service with a certain affectionate regard.

I wish to acknowledge my debt of gratitude to Mr. Merril Denison who gave me generously of his time and advice and assisted me greatly in completing this book.

WILLIAM GUY CARR

Toronto,
May, 1930.

BY GUESS AND BY GOD

CHAPTER ONE

To THE British, unlike the rest of the world, the capabilities of the submarine were no novelty. As early as 1904 a flotilla of A-boats accompanied the fleet on manœuvres.

Three hours after the outbreak of hostilities between Great Britain and Germany, two British submarines—*E-6,* Lieutenant Commander C. P. Talbot, and *E-8,* Lieutenant Commander F. H. Goodhart—carried out a reconnaissance in the Bight of Heligoland. Soon after, the thin white feather of a slowly moving periscope was sneaking in past the Island of Heligoland, and *E-9,* under command of Lieutenant Commander Max Horton, crept cautiously into the very harbour that the enemy High Seas Fleet used often as a base.

Commander Horton stood in the control room. Every now and then he issued orders: "Raise periscope!" "Stop!" "Lower periscope!" With the motors going dead slow ahead and the boat in perfect trim, he guided her into the narrow channel and made the harbour without being seen.

What would have happened to the British Fleet lying at anchor in Scapa Flow if the enemy had had officers on August 5th with the initiative of Horton, Boyle, Hughes, Nasmith, Laurence, Cochrane, to name a few?

Horton was disappointed. The periscope's mirror showed nothing worth wasting a torpedo on. For all the war craft in sight, Heligoland was still a peace-time harbour. Horton told the two anxiously eager officers beside him as much, and ordered the boat to the bottom. All hands were dismissed from stations for a rest. The three officers played bridge. Water is a good conductor of sound and all knew they would be sure to hear the propellers of any large vessel entering the harbour.

I heard the rest of the story months afterward. We were on patrol inside the Bight. Keeping watch with me on the conning tower was an old-timer of the Trade. The night was black. A sluggish roll sloshed the sides of the boat. The sea was empty. There was little to do save talk.

"It was somewhere's near here that the Trade inflicted its first defeat," said the lower rating. "But not on the enemy. We was dozing right in

Fritz's front dooryard with the gauges at sixty feet. Commander Horton, Mr. Chapman, and the navigating officer were playing bridge. Most of the hands were lying down reading. We could hear enemy ships scuttling about overhead, when sudden like I hears something clang against us away for'ard. The war hadn't been going long enough for us to know all we did later, as you might say, but it was plain to know what it was. They was sweeping, and their sweeps was hooked across our bows.

"I cups me head in me hand, wondering when the explosions would begin, when I hears the captain say, 'Your play, Chapman.' Mr. Chapman, I noticed, was a bit interested in this here row up for'ard too.

"The wire slipped and scraped. It was so plain you could see it all. Her skin might've been glass. The chains worked along the bow, scratched over the jumping wires, hitched up against the periscope standard, and after what seemed like a couple of weeks dragged clear. Just as it did Mr. Chapman says, 'Sorry, Horton old chap, but you are down one trick, doubled.'

"The captain laughs. A nasty laugh, it seems to me. 'Don't you believe it, Chapman,' he says. 'You revoked just when the wire hooked on. You forfeit two tricks.' Then he turns to the navigating officer who was keeping score, tells him what to put down, and says, 'Bridge, gentlemen, is a game you've simply got to keep your mind on if you ever hope to play it well.' "

Horton, with whom I served in the same flotilla for some months, never denied or confirmed the story, but officers seldom would comment on the lower deck's legends that grew up about them. But it's the sort of sailor story that is essentially truthful. Sailors seldom attempt to analyze character: they tell a story that illustrates it perfectly.

Nothing could give a better picture of the British submarine officers at the beginning of the war. They were young, they were already familiar with their boats, they had impudence born of sure courage, and in the tightest situations they kept their heads.

(2)

The British and German submarine services played exactly opposite rôles during the war. Where the Trade acted largely as eyes for the Fleet, the U-boats had no fleet to see for. Where the U-boat had to get out to kill, the Trade must go in to kill. The relative dangers are those a fly would risk in the lip and in the neck of a funnel. The farther the German submarine commander went the less frequent his difficulties: the farther the Britisher went the more dangerous his difficulties were certain to become.

So the epics of the Trade are those of penetrating the necks of two bottles, one in the south and one in the north: the entrance to the Sea of Marmora through the Dardanelles, and that of the Baltic through the Skagerrak. Their importance is obvious. The Baltic furnished the nearest contact with our Russian ally. Gallipoli was the horrible emphasis laid by the Allies on the importance of the Dardanelles.

The first boat to attempt the narrow channel separating Europe and Asia was *B-11* under command of Lieutenant N. Holbrook. Holbrook was a submarine officer of long experience. He was about twenty-five years of age. *B-11* was built in 1906. For her to have reached the Ægean under her own power seems surprising to those who think of the submarine as a product of this war. To expect her to penetrate the most difficult of sea-traffic routes seems now as ambitious as to expect to cross the Sahara in a 1909 Ford.

The straits leading from the Ægean to the Sea of Marmora are twenty-seven miles long and for three and a half miles of that distance are less than a mile wide. They change directions twice, at the Narrows between Kilid Bahr and Chanak from northeast to north, and at Nagara sharply from north to east. Currents from the Ægean and Black Sea rip through this narrow sea-way. In 1914 not too much was known about the sub-surface set and drift of these currents.

On December 13, 1914, *B-11* slipped away from the cover of the fleet with orders to torpedo anything he could find up the straits, and to report on the going. She poked her nose past Cape Hellas and Sedd-el-Bahr at the entrance, made the long reach to Kephez without being seen by the shore batteries, and dived under the five rows of mines off Kephez Bay and Point. Holbrook had no idea of his exact position and when he ran the periscope up for a look the first thing he saw was a large two-funnelled vessel painted gray and flying the Turkish ensign—the old battleship, the *Messudi-yeh*.

Closing up to eight hundred yards, he fired one torpedo and dived. As *B-11* slid under, the crew heard the explosion. Another peep with the periscope showed the Turk settling by the stern. She sank in ten minutes. Forced to the bottom by the hornet's nest of patrol boats aroused by the explosion, *B-11* considered the problem of getting home. She was worse than blind. Holbrook knew that he was somewhere between Kephez and the Narrows, but exactly where he wasn't sure. Judging by the land he had seen through the periscope, and figuring the time since he passed Sedd-el-Bahr, he judged he must be off Kephez Point. To add to the difficulties, the lenses of the spirit compasses had fogged and were useless.

Any thought of rising to get bearings was out of the question. The row above them told of the surface alive with craft. The first show of the periscope would have brought on a hurricane of shell.

Holbrook ordered full speed ahead, and steered in the direction he thought best. Several times the old boat bumped bottom but the risk of opening up her plates had to be run. When he judged that he must have passed under the mine fields, if his guess as to his direction was right, Holbrook came up to twenty feet, raised his periscope, and saw land on his port beam.

But the shore batteries, spaced less than a mile apart, kept him submerged until he was past Hellas on the way out. In all, the boat was under for nine hours, about all a crew could stand in a B-class submarine. By that time the air was so foul you couldn't burn a pine torch in her.

In the nine hours she sank an enemy battleship, dived under five mine fields twice, and navigated the Dardanelles though submerged and without a compass. Lieutenant Holbrook received the Victoria Cross, his second in command the D. S. O., and every member of the crew was decorated.

Following *B-11's* success another boat of the same class, the *B-9,* made the attempt, but was seen and forced to return with her plates badly loosened from the shelling she received.

(3)

The first British submarine to enter the Sea of Marmora, stay there at her own sweet will, and come out again was *E-14* under command of Lieutenant Commander E. Courtney Boyle. I served

with him in 1917 in the Blyth flotilla, and later
under him at Campbelltown on the west coast of
Scotland. Boyle was tall and dark with slightly
graying hair, very reserved and immensely self-
contained. Off duty, you would find him immersed
in some technical book or other most of the time.
He had a sense of humour but it never ran away
with him.

E-14 started through the Dardanelles as soon as
it was dark on the night of April 26, 1915. She
"proceeded on the surface using her engines."
Now in submarines the engines for running on the
surface were far from perfect. They had an appall-
ing habit of throwing out a smoke screen that made
many a destroyer jealous, and they were very far
from being noiseless.

As one lower-deck rating told me afterward:
"What with smoke belching out like a blooming
smelter, and the noise she made as we rattled along,
the Admiralty might as well've sent a brass band
ahead playing ' 'Ere the conquering 'eroes come.' "

She was seen. That goes without saying. Outside
the first mine field searchlights picked her up,
artillery got her range, and she was forced to dive.
It is impossible to see through a periscope in the
dark, so *E-14* had to stumble along blindly up the
straits trusting to her not-too-reliable compasses
to steer by.

Boyle had hoped, under the cover of darkness,
to creep through the obstructions he knew were

strewn in his path. Once the boat was forced under by the sweeping fingers of light thrown by the searchlights ashore, he had to take pot luck and keep going at a smart speed to keep the boat from getting out of hand in the strong currents.

The first bank of mine fields off Kephez was passed without much incident. The second was not so simple. They ran into it off Chanak where the sea-way is less than a mile wide and where the Turks had laid five tiers of floating death. The crew inside the boat could not tell where they were. Time and again they watched unseeing the scrape of wires and chains along her skin, as she tried to nose some way through submerged.

But it was impossible. Boyle ordered, "Surface stations," air hissed along the lines into the external tanks, and the conning tower broke water. They proceeded on the surface. They regulated their speed to make the run through the Narrows submerged at daybreak. The water was too calm for comfort. Every time the periscope was raised to get a bearing it was sighted by patrol boats and the shore batteries. The instant the tell-tale spume of white showed out in the channel surface craft dashed down on it, and the guns from both shores opened fire. For long hours the boat rested on the bottom waiting for quiet overhead.

It is hard to picture just what it was like for the men of the crew who could see nothing but who could hear the noise of thrashing propellers all around them, who could feel the jar of exploding shells, and who could only sense the tight corners they squeezed out of by hanging on to the sharp, terse orders issued by the pilot or their captain.

With all the forts firing, Boyle took *E-14* through near the surface, her periscope showing every few minutes. The water around her was churned almost white with the creamy wake of surface craft that tried to ram her. Shells rained down on her and one lucky shell crashed against the periscope and rendered it useless.

In the middle of this deadly game of hare and hounds, Boyle, using the other periscope, found time to attack and sink one of the larger Turkish gunboats. His report stated: "I just had time to see a great column of water shoot as high as the gunboat's mast when I had to dive again as some men in a small steamboat were leaning over the side trying to catch hold of my periscope. We dived and proceeded as requisite."

The dive took them under for six solid hours without a single chance of using their one eye, and they ran through the rest of the trouble as blind as kittens tied up in a sack.

Because they had been forced to use the power from their batteries extravagantly in order to dodge and shake off their pursuers, the interior of the boat became filled with the acid fumes off the batteries added to the smell of reeking oil. Finally they lost sound of the patrol boats and there was silence outside. They knew they must be out of the straits and actually in the Sea of Marmora.

Their batteries were almost done and the air in the boat was hardly fit to breathe. They were submerged for forty-five out of the first sixty-four hours.

(4)

Like the whale, a submarine must have air. She is in reality simply a destroyer which can hold her breath. But not forever. Although submersible, she must return at decent intervals to her own element and breathe. Not only does the air inside her acquire the foulness of something that has been used over and over again, but her batteries require recharging. Under water the boats run by electricity stored in huge batteries weighing half a ton each; on the surface they run by Diesel engines which live on small quantities of crude oil and enormous quantities of air. These Diesel engines in conjunction with dynamos also make the electricity which charges the batteries.

E-14's batteries were in bad shape. It was imperative that they be recharged, which meant coming to the surface. But the news that a submarine had succeeded in breaking through the elaborately protected straits and was somewhere loose in their private lake brought everything the Turks had to the west end of the Sea of Marmora. And in addition to all manner of things that floated, the shores were not so distant that a conning tower awash might not be spotted from them.

For twenty-four hours Boyle and his crew led the life of a weasel in a hen yard with the whole neighbourhood out hunting it. Again and again the boat came to the surface, got the desperate matter of charging the batteries under way, sighted the provoking hulk of a patrol boat, and was forced to dive. Each time she came up she was shelled by one or more destroyers, and with one periscope out of commission she was more than ordinarily sensitive about shelling.

Finding it hopeless to charge the batteries under these circumstances, she headed for the centre of the Sea of Marmora, where she found comparative peace. Here she remained, made juice for the hungry cells, and allowed all hands to see the sky.

On the 29th she started out to look for trouble along the Turkish main line of communications between Constantinople and the army operating against the Allies at Gallipoli. Early in the afternoon two troop ships convoyed by three destroyers came along. The sea was a sheet of glass; the periscope a magnet that drew every lookout's eyes. The destroyers turned and tried to ram her.

Boyle hung to the surface long enough to get the torpedo off at long range at one of the transports, but could not take a chance on observing the result of the shot. It was all right. A dull boom was felt after the proper interval; the black finger on the depth gauge fluttered. When he came up half an hour afterward a cloud of heavy smoke was billowing up from the transport, which had beached herself to prevent sinking.

Later that day he met the Australian submarine *AE-2,* which had preceded him into the Sea of Marmora. The Australian boat had come through the straits with great difficulty, had sunk a gunboat on the way through, and had run out of torpedoes. A meeting was arranged for the following day to transfer ammunition but it was never kept. A Turkish gunboat mortally wounded the Australian the next morning. To keep her from falling into the hands of the enemy, she was sunk by her commanding officer, Lieutenant Commander Stoker.

AE-2's short life was all hard luck. At Chanak going in she torpedoed a small gunboat, her compass developed defects, she ran aground under the guns of a Narrows fort, got off, ran aground again at Gallipoli and damaged her plates getting off. The next morning she attacked two men of war without success, entered the Marmora, sighted four transports, tried to sink one and the torpedo failed her. On the three successive days, till she met *E-14,* six different torpedoes failed to explode on their targets. On the 30th she was sent to the bottom.

E-14 carried on her weasel-like career during

the first four days of May. The weather was monotonously perfect. Patrol boats chased and har-
ried her, transports kept discreetly out of her way.
The lack of big game and the annoyance of small
craft that buzzed about her like horse flies seems
to have made her irritable. Lieutenant Commander
Boyle records in his report: "As I had not sighted
any transports lately, I decided to sink a patrol
ship as they were firing at me all the time."

The boat honoured proved to be a small mine
layer. She lasted less than a minute after the torpedo struck. A try was made for a larger one, but
in the clear water the wake of the tin fish was too
easily seen.

The first real chance came on May 5th, when
the *E-14* fell in with a large transport proceeding
toward the peninsula. She was under convoy of a
German-built destroyer capably handled. Using
his one periscope for split-minute looks, Boyle
waited until the zigzagging course of the destroyer
took her to the far side of the transport. As she slid
out of view behind the bulk of the troopship,
Boyle fired at six hundred yards. It was a clean
right-angle shot, with thirty seconds needed for
the torpedo to reach the victim. With the destroyer
screened there was no need to down periscope.
Twenty seconds, thirty seconds, forty-five seconds
passed. Nothing happened to disturb the progress
of the transport. The torpedo hit her and failed to
explode.

The following day another transport was sighted between Marmora Island and the south shore, but the submarine was discovered before she could close the distance to fire. The transport turned back to Constantinople.

May 10th was a profitable and interesting day. Early in the morning one of the German-built destroyers ran over her in the eastern part of the sea. During the day the usual number of steamers were chased, found crowded with refugees, and allowed to proceed on their way.

At sunset, when she was off the Island of Kalolimni, two large transports and a destroyer appeared in the direction of Constantinople. It was almost dusk when they were in position for the first shot. Again the torpedo failed, veering off its course and missing the leading transport.

The second ended the bad luck. It exploded. From the E-boat a fountain of surging smoke was seen to burst with the hit. Steel fragments, splintered wood, and men splattered into the sea. Night blanketed the wounded ship, and she was lost to those on board the submarine. They did not know her end till later.

She sank shortly after turning back on her course. The ship was the Turkish transport *Gul Djemal* carrying 6,000 troops and a battery of artillery to Gallipoli, and she had been armed with three-inch field guns to protect her from her vanquisher.

When I was serving with Commander Boyle in 1917 the *Gul Djemal,* although at the bottom of the Sea of Marmora, was of greater interest to the crew of *E-14* than when darkness shut her from their sight in May, 1915.

After learning who their victim had been, Boyle claimed "blood money" for the sinking. "Blood money" was the sum paid by the Admiralty to the crews of submarines for every member of the enemy they put out of action. If a submarine was fortunate enough to sink a battleship with a crew of 1,000 aboard, the Admiralty awarded the crew £5,000 to be divided amongst them. Five pounds for each enemy.

But this blood money was paid only when the vessel sunk was offensively armed. Commander Boyle claimed it on the grounds that the transport was armed with three-inch field guns, and that it was under convoy of a destroyer. A sound claim, it seemed to the Trade. The claim amounted to £30,000, five pounds for each Turkish soldier and sailor aboard her. The submarine's crew numbered about thirty officers and men. On an average each expected to receive about $5,000—a prodigious sum.

Long before the Admiralty had considered the claim, most of the crew had already spent their share. The *Gul Djemal* blood money, to men who thought in shillings, was an inexhaustible store of riches, to be drawn against for anything from buy-

ing an interest in a "pub" after the war to staging
a rousing binge during it.

When the Admiralty prize court considered the
claim it was turned down on the grounds that the
transport was defensively and not offensively
armed. To save most of his men from running foul
of the bailiff, Commander Boyle fought strenu-
ously in their behalf. The whole sympathy of their
comrades was with them, but the powers that be
said No. Many thought at the time that the decision was influenced more by the size of the claim
than by the technicality of the transport's armament. Thirty thousand pounds is a lot of money for
thirty men to split, and blood money was intended
as a reward—not a subsidy.

To return to the Marmora. After sinking the
Gul Djemal, E-14 was left with but one torpedo
and this turned out to be defective. With no gun
mounted, and with but a single periscope, there
was little she could do save create an impression.
This was exactly what she did. In Constantinople
she grew from one boat to a flotilla.

Armed with nothing but rifles, she prowled
around, stopping steamers and dhows and scaring
whom she could with rifle shots across their bows.
On May 15th she chased a small steamer ashore
near Panidos on the north shore. The beached crew
returned the insult with rifle fire, to which the
E-boat's crew replied with considerable relish.

Of the week he spent stalking with no more

armament than a deer hunter carries, Lieutenant Commander Boyle remarked upon the growing shyness of the enemy. A number of times enemy destroyers sighted him at close range in the dark. Although some were close enough to ram him had they wanted to, not one showed the least desire to do so.

On May 17th the boat was recalled by wireless. Her progress out of the Sea of Marmora and through the Dardanelles seemed like a mad procession. After diving all night she headed straight for Gallipoli, the north inside portal of the straits, chased by a two-funnelled gunboat, a torpedo boat, and a tug, one at each side and the other astern.

Diving under the first barrier near Nagara, she rose to periscope depth again off Chanak, followed the wake of an enemy patrol through the mine fields, passed a yacht, a battleship, and a number of tramps, ran through the Narrows under the fire of the Chanak forts, dived under the Kephez mine fields as before, and came to the surface near a French battleship after a twenty-one-day trip.

As would be expected, Lieutenant Commander Boyle reported that the success of *E-14* was due to his two junior officers, Lieutenant Edward Stanley and Acting Lieutenant Laurence, R. N. R. They received the D. S. C., and their commanding officer the Victoria Cross. He also received promotion to the rank of commander.

CHAPTER TWO

T HE departure of *E-14* from the Sea of Marmora meant no breathing spell for the nervous Turkish shipping in those placid waters. Within a few hours of her return to the fleet, a sister boat, *E-11,* was slipping through the Dardanelles with Constantinople itself as her avowed objective.

In command was Lieutenant Commander M. E. Nasmith, one of the most experienced submarine officers in the world. I served under him during the fall of 1917 when I was navigating officer of submarine *G-6* attached to the flotilla he commanded at Bantry Bay, Ireland. I knew also the two other officers: Lieutenant D'Oyly Hughes, whom I first met when I joined the submarine

service at Harwich, and the pilot, Lieutenant
Brown, R. N. R.

Nasmith was one of the most popular officers in
the British Submarine Service. A medium-sized
man, built and conditioned like a quarterback, extravagantly admired by his crews, affable and so-
ciable in the ward room, he had that rare combination, a delicate sense of the incongruous and an
almost ferocious insistence on efficiency.

In all, he spent three days less than one hundred
on his various trips into the Dardanelles. His
character explains the extraordinary things he
accomplished, as the manner of their accomplish-
ment explains his character. All of Nasmith's adventures had a flavour of their own. They were perfect. By that I mean the picture was complete.
Dumas would have added nothing, either of
daring, courage, skill, or impudence, to perfect
them as tales of high adventure.

Of the fury inefficiency aroused in him, I recall
a story of his first passage of the straits. *E-11* proceeded into the straits at 2:45 A.M. on the morning
of May 19th. Nine-forty-five saw her safely
through. The voyage was not unusual. Only seven
hours when the crew's nerves were like taut piano
wires.

When Nasmith attempted to report to the *Jed,*
a 550-ton destroyer at the other end of the Dardanelles, he found his wireless out of order and his
operator unable to repair it. The situation was a

very serious one. *E-11* had instructions to be on the lookout for signals during certain hours when she would receive instructions concerning the whereabouts of other British submarines and the activities of enemy vessels.

The fact that her wireless was useless upset the carefully laid plans. Nasmith called the crew together, held up the unfortunate wireless operator as an example of the danger one inefficient man can cause his comrades, of the menace he could be to the other boats of the flotilla, and of the detriment he was to the Allied cause.

Nasmith, the story went, with as many of the crew standing at attention around him as could gather in the control room, spoke his mind: "I consider a man of this type more deserving of the death penalty than the unfortunate individual who from work and fatigue drops asleep at his post of duty. Personally, I think I could forgive the man who fails in his duty because he falls a victim to outraged Nature. But a man who accepts a post of importance as the member of a submarine's crew knowing, as this man must have known, that he was not fully capable of meeting any emergency that might arise, either as a result of enemy action or ordinary wear and tear on his equipment, is a menace to his shipmates and a traitor to his cause."

It is hard to imagine a more devastating arraignment for a dereliction of duty, but if Nasmith did not spare his subordinate neither did he spare himself, for he added: "I am ashamed to confess that owing to my own inefficiency I am unable to tell this man how the repairs should be made."

His own efficiency was demonstrated a few days later when the Turks shot away the tip of his periscope in the Bosphorous. After finishing the work in hand Nasmith withdrew, came to the surface in a quiet spot, and repaired the damage.

The periscope is one of the most complicated instruments on board a submarine. The lenses and prisms can be put back in well over a thousand different combinations. Under ordinary circumstances, when repairs were required, a factory expert was sent to do them. Nasmith repaired his without any assistance while his crew took a bath in the Sea of Marmora.

(2)

Remembering the annoyance caused *E-14* by Turkish patrol boats, Nasmith captured a small sailing vessel soon after getting safely through the straits. Trimming the submarine down till only her conning tower was awash, he made his captive fast alongside. *E-11* was now, from the east, simply an innocent dhow which proceeded mysteriously on her way whatever the wind or lack of it. Behind this screen a hopeful lookout was kept for anything that floated, but the ruse was unsuccessful. Knowing of the crashing of the Narrows by another submarine, the Turk kept to his harbours. After a day of masquerade the dhow was turned back to her relieved crew, and Nasmith returned to the westward.

For two days nothing happened. Neither colour of sail nor smudge of smoke was sighted. It seemed as if *E-14's* conquests had cleaned the sea of traffic. On the 23d, however, the dull days ended. Early in the morning *E-11* was off Oxia Island, a few miles south of the entrance to the Bosphorus. A small dhow was sighted, and while busy with her an empty transport was sighted to the north, making for Constantinople. Forsaking the smaller prey for the larger, Nasmith gave chase.

The next hour was a thrilling one. The dhow had been sighted around 3:30 A.M., the transport sighted a little after four. Eight miles away lay Constantinople still hidden by the quickly loosening night. The water was deadly calm. The periscope dare split the sea for seconds only. Ahead was the ungainly transport; to the east, clarion colour waiting for the sun. At some one moment when he ordered "Raise periscope" Nasmith, his eye glued to the rubber eyepiece, must have seen the first level rays of sunrise crown the mosques and minarets with gold.

Around six the transport was abandoned for better quarry. A Turkish gunboat, *Pelenk-i-Dria,* was observed off Constantinople. *E-11* manœuvred for a shot, and loosed the port bow torpedo. It was a clean hit, and the Turkish sailors gamely manning

a six-pounder gun, opened fire on the contemptu-
ously raised periscope. It was here that the damage already mentioned occurred. The first round
hit the foremost periscope. An extraordinary shot.
Proceeding to *E-14's* preening ground off Kalolimni, the damage was repaired and the crew allowed a much-needed bath.

Communications were re-established with the
Jed on the 24th. Captain Nasmith's most cherished
story of his entire trip in the Sea of Marmora had
to do with an encounter on this day. Late in the
morning a small steamer was sighted and ordered
to stop. She ignored the order. *E-11,* having no
gun mounted, was forced to come to the surface
and rely on the dependable rifle. The effect of a
few rounds of small-arms fire was startling. The
crew took to the boats in a panic. Two were cap-
sized getting them into the water.

The crew of *E-11* cursed the crew for their
clumsiness, and lent a hand to help them right their
boats. During the confusion a sedate, calm figure
appeared on the upper deck. With a scrupulous regard for social etiquette he made no attempt to
speak until spoken to. Neither did he show the
least concern at being the one remaining person on
board. He was certainly no Turk.

When asked for explanations, he introduced
himself, "Silas Q. Swing of the Chicago *Sun,*" and
tendered his card over the ship's side to prove it.
He then objected to the inconvenience *E-11* was

causing him. Duty and a waiting world required
that he get to Chanak and find out what was happening there. Asked if the steamer had any supplies on board, he sensibly replied that he had no
idea what was on board. Nor did he give a damn,
it appeared.

Mr. Swing impressed Nasmith very much. He
always said that he must have been the world's
most unobservant journalist. "When D'Oyly
Hughes, my first lieutenant, went on board, the
first thing he saw was a six-inch gun lashed across
one of the hatchways. The mounting was located
in the forehold, and in the afterhold was a plentiful supply of ammunition to fit it. On deck were
cases marked 'Krupp.' " Mr. Swing was invited to
join the crew in the righted boats and forget about
Chanak. The waiting world would have to wait.
Hughes placed a demolition charge, and Swing
saw his means of transporation slide out of sight.

Before the swelling eddy of her going had
smoothed away they sighted the smoke of another
steamer, gave chase, and found her a store ship
heading for Rodosto, the largest Turkish port on
the north shore of the Marmora. She evidently
thought if she could make the harbour she would
be safe. But she wasn't. *E-11* came to the surface
and chased her till she was tied up alongside her
pier. With a gun it would have been a simple matter to finish her, but the submarine had no gun.
Nasmith submerged and discovered there was

none too much water to swim about in. She was hitting the bottom rather heavily, and he was forced to expose the periscope more than was healthy with the fire coming from the shore.

However, the ship was an important prize. Her decks were laden high with packing cases destined for troops on the peninsula. Luck was with Nasmith again. One successful shot and she broke into flames. The submarine, with her conning tower exposed at times because of the shallowness of the water, proceeded out of the bay.

Within ten minutes a third steamer was sighted. When ordered to stop she attempted to ram and, failing, ran for the shore, where she grounded. Here *E-11* had her first taste of the amphibian warfare she was later to become adept in. A demolition party was preparing to board the beached steamer when a party of Turkish cavalry appeared on the cliffs. Bullets rained down from above and Nasmith felt for once that discretion was the better part of valour.

(3)

Thanks to Silas Q. Swing, the rumour was already abroad in Constantinople that eleven British submarines were operating in the Sea of Marmora, when *E-11* herself arrived in the harbour. She was the first enemy of any description to intrude on the sacred precincts of the Golden Horn in the five hundred years the Turks had held the city. Na-

smith's own account is a classic of maddening
brevity. "So," he wrote, "we dived unobserved into
Constantinople." The word "so" refers to the dis-
gust the crew of *E-11* felt when they could find
nothing but small fry out in the open.

Nasmith raised periscope shortly after noon in
the centre of the harbour, and immediately there
occurred one of those incongruous incidents which
pleased him. "Our manœuvring," he used to say,
"was rather difficult because of the cross-tides, the
mud, and the current, but most particularly on account of a damn fool of a fisherman who kept trying to grab the top of my periscope every time I
raised it to take an observation. I don't think he
had any idea what it was, but to get rid of him I
gave him a chance to get a good hold on it. Then I
ordered 'Down periscope quickly' and almost
succeeded in capsizing his boat. When I looked at
him a minute later he wore the most amazed and
bewildered expression I ever hope to see."

The Arabian Nights Entertainment did not end
with the adventure of *E-11* and the modern Sind-
bad the Sailor. Rising close to the United States
ship *Scorpion*, a good-sized vessel was seen close
to the arsenal. Nasmith fired the port-bow tube.
The torpedo developed a gyro-failure, which
means that the gear which governed her direction
failed, locking the rudder hard over.

Nasmith said that the torpedo went chasing

around the harbour acting like nothing so much as a hen with its head cut off. Round and round it went at a speed of forty-seven knots, and every few seconds it switched from hen to porpoise and jumped out of the water. "It was bound to hit something, and by the look of things it was just as likely to be us as anything else."

So he fired the starboard-bow tube. By this time the harbour was in an uproar, and if ever a submarine was in a delicate position it was *E-11* at that moment. But Nasmith did a thing which I never heard equalled for sheer nerve. The moment he fired the torpedo at the ship loading by the arsenal wharf he put a small camera to the eyepiece of the periscope and took a picture of the munition ship blowing up. The first torpedo hit something and exploded at the same time.

"The enemy was given to issuing false reports about any successes we claimed," I have heard him explain. "They were experts at propaganda and counter-propaganda. So we could reap the full moral effect of going into their precious harbour and blowing their ships to hades as they laid moored safely inside, we tried taking some exposures with the camera lens close to the eyepiece of the periscope."

I saw the photograph. You could see the munition ship enveloped in a cloud of smoke with débris flying as high as the masthead. The sensitive film had also registered the cross wires and degree marks on the periscope lens which are used for judging distances and for taking bearings.

There was little question of the moral effect of *E-11's* astonishing exploit. Although the *Stambul* which she had sunk was an old ship, and was possibly beached before she sank, the city was thrown into a state of panic, troops were ordered off transports, and all sea traffic between Constantinople and the peninsula was virtually stopped.

Getting out of Constantinople was infinitely more exciting than getting in there. Once certain of his kill, Nasmith gave the order to dive. Down she sank and then grounded heavily.

"Then we bounced thirty feet, if the depth indicators were to be believed," to recall Nasmith's own story again. "I went down and sat on the bottom. Then a strange thing happened. We looked at the compass to discover our best course, and we noticed we were altering course rapidly even though we were right on the bottom. We were swinging right around the compass card. We watched this happening with great interest. It was evident that we must be resting on the shoal under Leander Tower, judging by the depth, and were being turned by the current unless something had succeeded in hooking on to us and was towing us. This was a disquieting thought, so we started the motors and bumped our way gently off the shoal, sank into about eighty-five feet of water, and proceeded as requisite out of the harbour."

And when they were safely out of the harbour and out of the narrow waters of the Golden Horn they headed for the quieter reaches in the centre of the Sea of Marmora by Kalolimni. Here they rested the next day, charged their batteries, and washed and bathed. Nasmith told me, and I know from experience, what a godsend it was to bathe and change into clean clothes.

(4)

All boats carried soap which would lather in salt water. Bathing consisted of stripping and jumping into the water while the watch kept a sharp look-out. As soon as you were wet you scrambled on board again, soaped yourself well, and washed off the lather with another quick dive into the briny. Clothes were laundered, using the steel decks as a washboard, and hung up on the jumping wires to dry.

After cleaning both boat and personnel, a good meal was usually prepared, minor repairs made which were considered necessary, and then the boat would be let down gently to the bed of the sea and all hands, save one man left as a guard, would turn in and sleep. So it was these crews lived for long periods, in one particular instance forty-eight days, before they took their lives in their hands again and attempted the passage of the Narrows.

And the food problem was not an easy one to solve. Some cooking could be done on the little

electric stoves, but it was impossible to keep good
anything that was not hermetically sealed. The
submarine owes its development to the Diesel engine, the storage battery, and canned goods. Without the latter, none of the endurance exploits of
either the British or German submarines would
have been possible. Canned goods, hard-tack, and
the blessedly ubiquitous rum were the chief items
on a submarine's menu. Drinking water was a
luxury indulged in only when one was really
thirsty. After a few weeks out the flavour didn't
make it appeal to you even when thirsty. As I have
already explained how we kept clean in hot
weather, there is no need to belabour the fact that
we stayed dirty in cold weather. It was impossible
to keep dry at any time.

In the Sea of Marmora the crews not only had
to be economical with their food and drink, but
with their torpedoes and ammunition as well.
Every shell had to find a billet, every torpedo its
mark. The problem of food and drink was the
comparatively simple one of rationing. Perhaps
fortunately, the air in a submarine did not induce
ravenous appetites. But the problem of guarantee-
ing each torpedo a bull's-eye was not so simple.

It was the practice in the Trade to set all torpedoes to sink if they missed their targets. This
prevented their falling into the hands of the enemy
or constituting a menace to navigation which
would endanger enemy, Allied, and neutral ship-

ping alike. A live torpedo when set to float is nothing more or less than a huge mine and almost as dangerous.

Commander Nasmith agreed that this practice was sensible when a depot ship was handy to supply you with all the "tin fish" you required, but with the Dardanelles between him and fresh supplies he concluded the practice could be modified. He therefore adopted the expedient of setting his torpedoes to float, and, if he missed a shot, he waited until his intended victim had gone on its way, and then retrieved the torpedo at his leisure. "Tin fish which fight and run away must live to fight another day" seems to have been his reading of the old proverb.

The first chance to try this conservation policy came on the 28th. After sighting a convoy of six ships early in the morning and sinking the largest, he ran in with a steamer bound for Constantinople from Panderma, the railway port on the south shore. The vessel was a long way off, and so located that he couldn't manœuvre to get closer. Setting his torpedo to float, he tried the long shot and missed.

E-11 waited until the steamer had disappeared to the north, and prowled around till she found the big cylinder of floating death. The top of the head was grazed but the pistol was not discharged, showing that it had missed the keel by inches. Nasmith was now faced with the problem of get-

ENEMY GUNNERY

This is a close-up photograph of the periscope
of the *E-11* after Nasmith returned from his
exploits in the harbour of Constantinople.

ting his torpedo back into its tube. The accepted
method was to hoist them aboard from the depot
ship by means of a derrick. There was no derrick
on *E-11*.

Nasmith blew the water out of her for'ard tanks,
and then flooded the after tanks until the boat's
bows were raised sufficiently to bring the torpedo
tubes just level with the water. The rear doors of
the tube inside the boat were then closed, the bow
cap opened, and a couple of the crew jumped
overboard. Swimming one on either side, they
steered the "fish" tail first into its tube. The bow
cap was closed, the boat rimmed, water drained
from the tube, the rear doors opened, and the torpedo hauled into the for'ard compartment for recharging and overhauling. The new plan had
proved itself. It was simple, easily accomplished,
and was used successfully a number of times.

To conserve their torpedoes further, Nasmith
resorted to other economies. He had no gun, and
he disliked wasting precious tin fish on the dhows
which were continually plying between the shores
of Asia Minor and Turkey in Europe. What he
did was to chase them on the surface, come alongside, and force them to surrender. The crew would
then be taken aboard *E-11,* and the small sailing
boat burned. Another one sighted, the same process would be repeated. When the submarine had
collected more passengers than she could accommodate, they were transferred to a captured boat,

and a course was set for them to the nearest harbour. Occasionally the routine varied. When a fleet of sailing craft was found, the crews were transferred to one of the boats, the rest tied together and burned. Demolition charges were saved for bigger game. But always the crews were taken care of. Not a single noncombatant lost his life through the operations of our submarines in the Sea of Marmora.

E-11 had now been nine days in and big game was growing very scarce. For two days more she prowled around like a hungry tiger, and found nothing but dhows. These were certainly profitable, and always amusing, but hardly satisfying. As a result, Nasmith dived and proceeded into Panderma Roads. It was here that he found one of the latest vessels of the Rickmers Line, and torpedoed her. She was towed ashore in a sinking condition.

Having received word from the *Jed* of troop movements between Ismid, the port at the eastern tip of the Marmora, and the north shore, *E-11* spent the rest of the day watching the eastern transport route without success, but the very difficulty the boat was experiencing in finding anything to attack was the best possible guarantee of her success.

But June 2d was a big day. After communicating with the *Jed*, *E-11* proceeded toward the northern transport route, and sighted a ship to the eastward. The boat dived, and got in a clean hit on the steamer's port side. The explosion was tremendous. A quivering instant after the torpedo hit, the entire upper deck was lifted overboard. She had been filled with munitions.

An hour later the port-beam tube was fired at a small store ship, and, missing her, ran on toward a small town. The crew of the steamer took her into shore and landed. *E-11* moved in to finish her with a demolition charge but was driven off by rifle fire. Less than two hours later two destroyers were sighted in company with a dispatch boat. Unseen by the destroyers, a torpedo was sent on its way, and missed. This one was recovered later and passed in through the tubes.

After two comparatively inactive days an examination of the mechanical equipment showed the terrific strain the boat had been under during her seventeen days of gentlemanly raiding. One motor was badly damaged and one of the driving shafts was cracked. Nasmith thought it advisable to return. June 6th was spent charging batteries and resting, and at 10 P. M. she proceeded as requisite for Gallipoli.

(5)

It is hard to imagine that any fitting climax could be managed to round out *E-11's* cruise. What more astonishing thing was there left her than she had already done? After the tumult in Constantinople it seems that anything must be an anticlimax. But not with Nasmith in command. As I have said of his adventures, each seems a work of art, and perfect in its way.

Thanks to her recaptured tin fish, *E-11* still had two loaded tubes. These were being saved for the battleships stationed above the Narrows, which Nasmith was confident of finding on his way out.

Gallipoli was passed at about one hundred feet, and *E-11* proceeded toward Nagara, coming up at regular intervals to examine all anchorages for first-class fighting ships. This was to be the climax —the sinking of a Turkish dreadnought.

Slowly she poked her nose down the Dardanelles. Time and again the periscope was raised, swung hopefully through the arc, and drew a blank. Eight miles above Nagara Point a large empty transport was sighted anchored close to shore. Her position was noted and nothing more. The torpedoes were for bigger things. The boat reached Nagara and still nothing had been seen. The three officers were not discouraged. Beyond Nagara, where the straits swing sharply to the south, they would certainly find battleships.

Nagara was passed on their port side, and they, unseen, headed down the narrowing straits toward Chanak and the Narrows. Off Chanak, close to the first mine field, nothing had been seen. At the threshold of escape, with nearly three weeks of astonishing deeds behind her, there seems to have been no question as to what *E-11* should do next.

Nasmith ordered the helmsman to turn sixteen points, and she doubled back on her track, past Nagara, on to Moussa Bank where the empty transport lay in wait. She was torpedoed, and *E-11* continued her journey down the straits.

With a clear conscience, Nasmith headed for home in earnest. Nothing is mentioned in the boat's official log of the hundred and one dangers she knew she escaped, and the thousand and one dangers she escaped and knew nothing of, but I can remember a member of the crew telling what really happened. It seems to me, knowing submarines, the real climax of the story.

"Just as we got off Kilid Bahr something happened," he told me. "The boat got out of trim. Don't know to this day what got hold of her, but suddenly she started for the surface. Now, we daren't give our position away because patrol craft were as thick as fleas on a dog. Besides, by this time we knew of the torpedo tubes they had rigged up ashore on both sides of the Narrows, and we also knew they had set observation mines which they could explode from the shore if they got one glimpse of our periscope as we made our way through.

"As I say, I don't know what happened to make her rise, but we had to flood every tank in her to keep from breaking surface. It may have been a sudden change in the density of the water, it may have been anything, but no sooner had we got her down and under control again than she did just the opposite and started to take a dive. She was down to depths greater than her builders ever intended her to go before we got the ballast water out of her and started coming up again."[*]

Having extracted themselves from this delicate situation, they next heard a noise as though they had grounded. This was impossible when no bottom was near. There was nothing for it but to find out the cause of the grating and the boat was brought up to twenty feet. The periscope was raised—reluctantly enough, I should say. As soon as the periscope was clear an ominous bulk was seen pushing on ahead. A mine had fouled evidently on their for'ard port hydroplane.

No less welcome companion could be imagined. A roll, a lurch, a slip in the fouled chain, and one of the delicate horns would have made contact. They dared not come to the surface to disengage it because of the batteries ashore, and so they proceeded pushing the engine of death ahead of them until they got as far as Kum Kaleh. For well over an hour the crew lived an exquisite nightmare expecting some one of the crawling seconds to be the last they would ever know.

Outside the entrance to the straits Nasmith undertook the infinitely delicate task of clearing her.

[*]The author had a similar experience in the entrance to the Baltic and is convinced that the strange behaviour of *E-11* was due to her encountering strata of water with greatly varying degrees of density. The effect is much the same as when an airplane runs into air pockets and for the same reason.

First he emptied his after tanks, which allowed her bows to sink. Then he ordered full speed astern on the motors. In this position the boat rose to the surface. The sternway gathered and the rush of water from the screws swept the mine away from her bows.

Shortly after she was met by the British destroyer *Grampus* and escorted into Mudros. In addition to the moral effect of her cruise, she had sunk two ammunition ships, two store ships, two troop ships, a number of sailing vessels, and beached a third transport with a gaping hole in her.

As in the case of Holbrook and Boyle, Lieutenant Commander Nasmith received the Victoria Cross, and his officers and crew were proportionately decorated.

CHAPTER THREE

B OYLE'S and Nasmith's daring forays into the
heart of Turkish waters were not allowed to stand
as isolated examples of the prowess of the Trade.
Having proved the Dardanelles pregnable by two
successful trips, our boats exploited their confidence with scheduled assurance. Boat succeeded
boat with clockwork regularity. The barriers were
crashed, rendezvous kept, patrols made. Nasmith
came out on June 7th; Boyle took *E-14* in on June
9th. *E-12* joined her June 19th, and was relieved
by *E-7* on June 30th. During July Boyle brought
E-14 out, and took her in again on the 21st. He was
joined early in August by Nasmith. Later in the
month *E-7* returned, and Boyle was relieved by
E-2 under Commander David Stocks. In Septem-

ber two new boats, *E-20* and *H-1* joined the hunting.

Every boat accomplished the incredible. Every crew added new chapters to the story of the sea. To detail all their adventures would require much space, and since even thrills become monotonous, it is only possible to deal with the high lights of succeeding voyages, and particularly those of boats not already introduced. For this reason, Boyle's second trip with *E-14* is passed over in order to tell the story of *E-12*.

This boat made two trips into the Sea of Marmora under Lieutenant Commander Bruce, remained forty days on the second and fell into as many hair-raising adventures as any submarine operating in Eastern waters. Bruce and his crew first tackled the Narrows on June 19, 1915. It was the most desperately perilous passage made up to that time. Halfway through *E-12* became almost hopelessly entangled in the nets and obstructions which the Turks were continually adding to their defenses.

Hoping to spare his motors, Bruce tried to coax the boat out of her trouble. Gentleness proved utterly unavailing. It was not a situation for nosing through. It was crash or nothing. Flooding all tanks, he forced the boat to drop like a stone. As she sank, he drove her alternately astern and ahead, using every ounce of power her motors would deliver. After rocketing back and forth like a great fish lashing herself free from a net, she lunged ahead dragging the obstructions with her. But a terrific strain had been put on the motors, and the record of Bruce's patrol shows them developing defects almost all the time. With this handicap he succeeded in sinking thirty-four vessels, attacked and destroyed several ammunition dumps, and shelled the railway line by which the Turks were moving troops and supplies to the Gallipoli front.

The red-letter day of his first patrol was June 25th. In the morning he had a run in with two steamers and five sailing vessels they were towing. Owing to the damage to her motors, *E-12* did most of her work on the surface. She closed to within a reasonable distance of the first steamer and ordered her to heave to. Careful scrutiny failed to reveal anything of a suspicious character. She was apparently unarmed, and the crew were all on deck in life belts. Bruce ran alongside and ordered his first lieutenant, Tristram Fox, to board her. To save ammunition, they intended to sink the steamer by setting fire to her and opening her sea cocks. Ammunition was reserved for the more satisfying business of shelling enemy troops on shore.

When they were close alongside it was seen that the steamer carried no small boats. Fox, followed by a couple of men, scrambled aboard the intercepted vessel. Just as they reached the deck, a Turk heaved a bomb down on the deck of the submarine. It hit *E-12* forward, and bounced off the steel deck

without exploding. It was the only bomb thrown.
Immediately the boarding party drew their revolvers. Fox's position was a very delicate one. He
saw that the Turks meant fight, and he knew that
his own boat would open fire at any second. On the
steamer a small gun mounted aft opened fire, and
rifles spattered lead from concealed positions.

While Fox and his men were fighting for their
lives on the deck of the steamer, Bruce coolly set
about the job of sinking her. Charles Case, the
coxswain, formed himself into an ammunition
hoist for *E-12's* light gun. The crew shot steadily
through a rain of rifle and gun fire at a range of
thirty feet. The gun crew fired at point-blank
range into the stern of the enemy, and having si-
lenced her gun, methodically placed ten shots in
her from bow to stern.

The dog fight seemed to be *E-12's,* when the two
sailing vessels in tow tried out a brainy move on
their own. They came in on the submarine's flank,
opened fire with rifles, and tried to foul her propellers. Clever manœuvring kept the submarine
close up against the steamer, and the conning tower
between the gun crew and the sailing ships which
had started to take a hand in the mêlée. With her
back literally to a wall, *E-12* fought off the two on
her flank, and turned her attention to the steamer
again. It was soon beaten. Bruce drew off and sank
all three of them.

In his official report he told of this scrap laconically and mentioned that "our one workable motor unfortunately developed slight defects." He also considered "it worth while to mention the first lieutenant's behaviour under very trying circumstances." The trying circumstances being that Fox and his party were not only under enemy fire but also under fire of their own men, and they were still aboard the Turkish ship fighting when the ammunition in the forward hold blew up as the result of *E-12's* shell fire. He also commended the coxswain and the gun's crew. "They did very well considering," he said. Considering what? one wonders. "Considering," he continued, "they were under rifle fire and the shells from the one-inch gun fired at a range of nine yards."

Having disposed of one convoy, *E-12* at once turned her attention to the other. The second had sensibly devoted herself to the business of escape. When Bruce cast around for her she was already well away toward the shore. *E-12* gave chase and opened fire at two thousand yards. Two shells from his puny gun found their mark, one forward and one aft. Fire broke out forward. To better her speed, the steamer slipped her tow and left the three dhows easy victims to the pursuing submarine. *E-12* ignored them, and drove on until she forced the larger quarry to beach herself. Troops ashore then joined the duel, and opened fire with a large-calibre gun. Having accomplished her purpose, *E-12* withdrew to toil over her troublesome motors.

Of *E-12's* second journey in October much could be told. She prowled around for forty days, sometimes alone, sometimes in company with *H-1* and the ill-fated *E-20*. Together she and the H-boat harassed a gunboat off Kalolimni as marauding wolves pull down a deer. Alone she carried out successful target practice on a powder factory near Constantinople. Like all the boats, she worried Turkish shipping in much the same manner as a terrier worries old shoes.

But the greatest of her experiences came on her way out. Many a boat would have returned to her base long before she did. Her motors were a continuous source of trouble and anxiety. She could use only one when diving. Had this one failed her she never could have reached home. But she carried on until her last torpedo tube was empty and her ammunition fired at worthwhile targets. Then, and only then, did Bruce head her for the outside.

Again she got entangled in new nets on her way out. Using the lashing tactics that had served her before, Bruce fought her free. She took a good part of one obstruction with her, dangling like a hangman's noose from her bows. Burdened with this extra weight, the boat began to sink quietly to the bed of the channel. Slowly the hands of the depth gauges registered increasing pressures. One hundred, two hundred feet she settled.

Bruce sought every desperate means to hold her fall. He blew her bow tanks and drove her full speed ahead. Even in this position she continued slowly to sink. As if to drive the struggling crew to despair, the forward hydroplanes jammed and the electrical gear went out of business. Down she went to 245 feet. At such a depth she was an eggshell in a slowly closing fist. The conning-tower scuttles broke inward under the tremendous pressure. The conning tower flooded with water. Forward plates weakened and she leaked badly. The doors of the forward compartment were closed to keep the water from seeping into the batteries. Once it reached them, deadly chlorine gas would be produced.

Death seemed actually to be knocking at the hull of the boat. Bruce kept his head. The hydroplanes were put into hand gear, and three men put to work on them. Their superhuman efforts gained a little elevation on the horizontal rudders. Suddenly the boat lunged upward with a terrific rush. The three men on the gears fought desperately to depress her fins. At fifty feet they had made an impression. At twelve she paused and settled back to fifty, but not soon enough to keep her hidden from six patrol boats following on the surface the wake of her entanglement. Inside the boat they could hear shells bursting above them. The concussion of a hit was felt, and light bulbs and delicate instruments were broken.

Still the crew remained steadily at their stations waiting calmly to carry out whatever orders their commander might see fit to issue. Trying to get out of the way of the shell fire from the patrol boats, *E-12* crashed down again at a sickening angle to below 200 feet again. The gyro compass had been rendered useless. The magnetic compasses had been smashed by the shell that entered the conning tower. The depth gauges refused to register. The boat was headed blindly in the direction her officers thought salvation lay. They certainly went by guess and by God.

And as she plunged blindly down the straits, not knowing what new terror she might encounter, the crew felt her run solidly into another obstruction. To the men imprisoned inside her, the sounds were those of chains scraping along her hull. They waited breathless moments wondering what the new threat meant. Perspiration stood in great beads on their foreheads. None spoke except to ask or answer a question, or to repeat, according to the custom of the service, an order given by one of the officers.

The power in the batteries was almost exhausted and the atmosphere in the boat foul. It was also humid and warm. The gas from overheated batteries bit on the men's tongues with an acid tang. Their breath came heavy and laboured. Each man fought to keep his eyes expressionless. I heard the story of that trip down the straits from one of the

men who had served in *E-12* at that time. It was a
tale of unbelievable control in the face of immi-
nent death by men apparently without a fighting
chance for life.

Throughout it all Bruce remained cool and cal-
culating, a master of the situation like a rider on
an unbroken horse that has not thrown him yet.

Checked by the last obstruction, he marked the
side of impact, and worked his helm hard away
from it. Then he demanded a last desperate show
of power from the failing motors. As he ordered
full speed ahead, the new entanglement was heard
to slide along the hull, and as it did it cleared her
of the old one that had caused all their trouble.

Suddenly relieved of the great weight of wire
and chains, the boat rose steeply by the bow and
broke surface. Patrol boats and shore batteries
were waiting for her, shells splashed around her.
One hit the conning tower; two others hit the
bridge; two torpedoes fired from tubes ashore sped
a few feet by her stern. By some miracle of luck
and skill and nerve she came safely through to
the protection of the fleet. Friendly destroyers
escorted her to her base after a cruise of more than
two thousand miles.

(2)

Some idea of the risks run by the crews of submarines operating in the Sea of Marmora is given
by the fact that none of the five French boats de-

tailed to this work survived. In addition, the British lost four boats, two attempting the passage of the Dardanelles, and two in the Marmora. While the veteran raiders of the inland sea, Boyle and Nasmith, took their boats through the mine-infested channel, and other commanders made passages which they described as "without any special incident," there was not a single boat which escaped some one remarkable experience while forcing her way past Nagara.

Typical of these is the adventure that befell *E-2* when she made her first trip up in August, under the command of Lieutenant Commander Stocks, to take the place of *E-14*. She was one of the older E-boats. On her way through the Narrows she became badly entangled in wire and nets which fouled her gun mounting, the conning tower, and the wireless standard. To extricate himself from this mess, Stocks opened the dead lights on the conning tower and surveyed the situation at a depth of about sixty feet.

Staring into the dark, greenish glow of the waters at that depth, Stocks sensed that the boat was held by tentacles of wire rope. Half a turn of $3\frac{1}{2}$-inch wire had caught below the gun, and around the conning tower was a full turn of smaller rope. While he was debating how to clear the boat, a series of small explosions told the crew that on the surface patrol boats knew of their predicament and were dropping bombs down on them.

These bombs may have been her salvation. For the ten minutes *E-2* plunged with all her force to free herself, the explosions continued. Some of them must undoubtedly have broken or cut the strands of wire which held the boat imprisoned. Suddenly she wrenched herself away and proceeded as requisite, accompanied on the surface by a trailing destroyer which shelled her periodically as she took a peep through her periscope.

In' freeing herself, she badly strained her hull, particularly under the gun mounting. So serious was the damage that *E-2* was a miserable leaky boat for the whole of her thirty-one-day cruise. Her first job was to make repairs and keep a rendezvous with *E-11* for the delivery of a fresh supply of ammunition. In the centre of the Marmora where things were decently quiet Stocks and Nasmith kept their appointment, and exchanged news. *E-11* went off about her business, and *E-2* dressed her wounds.

It was necessary to unship the old gun from its original mounting. There were two reasons. First because the bolts which held it on its seating had been sheered off when the boat crashed from the obstruction, and second because rivets had been started and were leaking badly below the mounting. Firing from its old seating, the gun made the boat leak so greatly that it was impossible to dive to any great depth. Increased pressure forced water into her in dangerous quantities.

With her gun newly mounted—and that short phrase does scant credit to the days of hard work that went into the business—*E-2* started on the warpath. She sank steamers and burned dhows, and was worried in return by torpedo boats and enemy aircraft newly introduced to stem the impudent successes of our boats. From time to time she met *E-11* at the preening ground and together they went off on duel hunts.

Her crew were born gunners. They seemed to delight in fighting duels with guns ashore. To discover these guns, they chased enemy shipping, which naturally sought the protection of the temporary land forts. Then it was a simple matter to locate the gun. All they had to do was watch where the shells came from. I remember one of the Dardanelles officers sarcastically remarking that he had run into one of these guns unawares, and that it had held its fire until his boat was uncomfortably close. "But they missed us, as usual," he said. It is only fair to point out that they did not always miss. At least one of our boats and two French submarines fell victims to the accuracy of their aim.

So addicted was *E-2* to brawls with field artillery that it was necessary to change the gun mounting a second time. In her records is the statement: "When there was nothing else doing we were mostly working on the gun." After changing the mounting she assisted *E-11* in a joint bombardment of a magazine and railway station at Mudania, a port on the south shore opposite Constantinople.

This was on August 25th. It was on this day that *E-2's* crew heard from the men of *E-11* the story of the most daring single adventure of the E-boats' Marmora days. A few nights before, D'Oyly Hughes, *E-11's* first lieutenant, had swum ashore and blown up a railroad bridge. The recital fired the ambition of *E-2's* second in command to do the same.

Lieutenant Lyons was a good swimmer. On September 7th he swam from his boat and destroyed two dhows. Later that day preparations were made for his great adventure. The next morning, long before dawn, he slipped quietly into the water and pushed ahead of him a light raft carrying a demolition charge, his revolver, and his clothes.

His brother officers watched him until he disappeared into the night. They lost sight of him when he was less than one hundred yards from the boat. The night was black and still. From the shore noises could be distinctly heard. The officers awaited anxiously the sound of an explosion, or the single pistol shot that would tell them Lyons was in trouble. Given it, they were to fire on the railroad station.

Minutes dragged out into an hour. How slowly only those who stood there on the conning tower, staring into the darkness and straining their ears for every sound, will ever realize. Another hour crawled by and then another, each one longer than the last. Day began to dawn. With dawn came the sound of a devastating explosion. But no signal came from Lieutenant Lyons. It was broad daylight. *E-2* and her loyal crew still clung to their desperate hope that Lyons would yet return. Commander Stocks held his boat as long as he dared— probably longer.

Shortly after 7 A. M. he was forced to sea. An hour later saw him back again cruising on the surface. He thought that Lyons might have secured a small boat, and would be found drifting somewhere off shore. The next day at dawn *E-2* came again, still hoping. But no small boat was seen, nor was Lyons ever heard of again.

Nor has the mystery ever yet been solved of how or why he disappeared so completely. That his courage was rewarded seems proven by the explosion heard aboard *E-2* at dawn. What happened to him is left to conjecture. He was not captured. Did he find his objective guarded and wait patiently for the chance to place his charge of guncotton? Was he finally discovered, and, knowing himself hopelessly outnumbered, did he light the charge, and stand guard over the spluttering fuse? Did he protect the charge from interference until overpowered, and then die with his captors as the explosion blew them all into eternity?

No one knows. It never will be known what happened in the chilly hours of that early dawn. But

from what I heard from Lyons' brother officers
and men, I believe that what I have suggested is
possibly very near the truth.

Short one officer, with a boat leaking so that the
crew often had to man the hand pumps, on short
allowances of drinking water, Stocks kept *E-2* at
work another six days. In that time she limped
around concerning herself mainly with dhows, for
by this time there was little else to be found any-
where in the Sea of Marmora. The same scrupulous regard for noncombatants guided Stocks's actions as had guided those of the other gentlemen
raiders of the Sea of Marmora.

The men kept their tempers. They practised no
frightfulness. Often, when they considered a sinking necessary, they took the crew on board and
kept them aboard until they could land them at
some village, or put them aboard another boat. In
this work there was more of humour than terror. I
remember one of the navigating officers with whom
I served at Blythe who used to delight in telling
stories of carnival captures among the Turks.

"To save ammunition," he once said, "we would
round up a dozen dhows. The crews would be lined
up on the deck of the sub, where every man,
woman, and child had a splendid view. Then we
tied all the dhows together, bow to stern, in the
form of a rough circle. The next step was to set
fire to them. When they were burned to the water's
edge our prisoners would stand puzzled and wor-

ried to know what fate was in store for them. We always put them aboard the next dhow we captured and sent the crowd of them to the nearest port. Some left us with what we hoped were expressions of good will, and others plainly cursed us with all the venom they could command."

E-2 had one more piece of bad luck to face before she took her chances with the death traps that floated between her and her base. Fuel oil leaked into her main fresh-water supply. The men had to be put on the most meagre rations, and the last pint was actually served out while they were forcing their way through the Narrows. "And if there was ever a place a man needed a drink, it was there," a lower-deck rating told me, adding cryptically, "Your mouth got so awful dry."

And not without reason. Crashing through the nets, *E-2* damaged her hydroplanes and finally smashed off one of them. More leaks developed. The men manned the pumps with desperate anxiety. Part sieve, part submarine, and manned by a parched and weary crew, she rose to safety inside her own patrols.

CHAPTER FOUR

T HE work of British boats in the Sea of Marmora
was of great service to the Allied armies battling to
retain their toe hold on Gallipoli. What the British Grand Fleet had done to German shipping,
British submarines in a few mad forays did to
Turkish. By mid-July, shipping in the Marmora
was virtually paralyzed. Transports kept to their
harbours. All battleships were moved above the
second bridge of the Bosphorus to keep them out
of harm's way. Supply ships resigned their duties
to dhows which moved timorously by night under
heavy convoy. Troops bound for the front were
forced to keep to land. In place of a short, simple
journey by water, they moved by rail to Rodosto,

and then marched three days inland over hot, dusty roads.

As a result the adventures of the E-boats inside the Dardanelles began to take on a different character. Denied ships, their natural enemies, they were forced to strange amphibian undertakings. There were brawls with cavalry, gun duels with field artillery, strafes on marching troops. Their military object being to harass the Turkish communications, they did not stop when they had accomplished their purpose on water; they took to the land. Prowling along the shore between Stefano and Ismid, where the Berlin-to-Bagdad railroad ran, they shelled troop trains, railway stations, and ammunition dumps. So completely did the E-boats hold control of the Marmora that, save for going in and out, they acted more as monitors than submarines.

To *E*-7 (Lieutenant Commander Cochrane) went the credit for first giving serious attention to the land. Other boats had been embroiled defensively with shore parties: *E*-7 took the offensive.

Cochrane took her on her first trip through the Dardanelles on June 30th. She had the usual experiences going up. She plunged deep under the mine fields; staggered through the nets. Death scratched with iron fingers on her steel plates; the clang of metal striking hollow metal sounded menacingly within her. A destroyer picked up her track and diligently followed. Twice when she came up for a look she escaped ramming by scant feet. The destroyer told the shore where she could be found, and a torpedo from a shore tube passed between her wireless standards. All as requisite, she proceeded on her way until she kept her rendezvous next evening with *E-14* at the "town pump" off Kalolimni.

Next day Cochrane set to work. In the morning a small steamer was captured. A boarding party was sent to sink her. A demolition charge was placed in her hold and the fuse took light but the explosion was premature. Lieutenant Halifax and one of the crew were so badly burned that neither of them was of service for the rest of the voyage. Burns under any circumstances are horrible; imagine enduring them for three July weeks in the interior of a submarine. In addition to these casualties, the other two officers and the wireless operator were stricken with dysentery.

Only one who has actually known for himself the abomination of life aboard a submarine can have any conception of what the men on *E*-7 went through on their three weeks' voyage.

Despite a truly horrible physical handicap, they carried on. In ten days they sank two sailing vessels, two steamers, and a number of dhows. On July 10th they discovered the 3,000-ton *Biga* alongside the pier at Mudania. Screening her were a number of sailing ships. Cochrane dived under these, came up between them and the *Biga,* and launched a torpedo at her. The explosion was unusually heavy.

The next adventure came a few days later. On the night of the 15th, while prowling around the entrance to the Bosphorus, *E*-7 ran aground on the shoal off Leander Tower. To improve the shining hour, a torpedo with a TNT head was fired into the arsenal. At the proper interval a violent explosion was heard, but there was no chance to find out its results. Freeing herself from the shoal, *E*-7 next moved out into the Bosphorus and shelled powder mills on the western outskirts of Constantinople.

The success of this midnight bombardment must have been the inspiration for Cochrane's next move. On the 17th he turned up at the mouth of the Gulf of Ismid where the railroad line from Scutari passes close to the sea. At one point there is a deep cut. *E*-7 devoted her attentions to this spot, shelling it until the railroad line was blocked.

And then, as I remember a story I heard more than once, they lingered, hoping for a train. None appearing, impatience beset them, and they started off down the coast to find one. At Derinji they paused to examine a closed shipyard and while there sighted a troop train bound toward Constantinople. Absurdly they set off at full speed down the gulf in a crazy race after the train. It outdistanced them of course, but they tore hopefully ahead. Within thirty minutes they were rewarded by seeing the train returning slowly. It seemed to be seeking some secluded spot where it might stop. Off shore Cochrane watched it. The train entered a stand of timber. There was a tense wait to see if it would appear at the other side. Minutes passed. Nothing happened. It appeared definitely to have stopped. The gun crew were ordered to action stations. The target hidden, there was no chance to spot their hits. But the genius of the Trade is to reach unseen objectives. After a couple of dozen rounds three ammunition cars blew up.

The flavour of this strange new game appealed strongly to *E*-7. During the last week of her voyage she returned again and again to the line skirting the north shore of the Gulf of Ismid. At the scene of her first success she caught another train and gave it a sound shelling. She spent unprofitable hours shelling the viaduct that was to be the scene of amazing daring a few days later. She shelled another moving train. But more than all else, she demonstrated the weakness of the Turk's main line of communications with Asia Minor. Thus did each new boat to range the Sea of Marmora add to the achievements of her predecessors.

E-7 and her dysentery-weakened crew returned to their base on July 24th, after meeting with *E-14* from whom they learned of new nets across the Narrows, and to whom they told of the activities along the railroad.

(2)

Early in August the work of the Trade in the
Sea of Marmora took on a new phase. The boats
began to work in pairs, and in place of acting in-
dependently to harass Turkish communications
they operated jointly with the army in the desperate attempts being made to break the stalemate on
Gallipoli. Theirs were possibly the greatest successes won by the naval forces in the vast amphibi-
ous undertaking.

The two boats to work first as a team were the
veterans *E-14* and *E-11*. Boyle with *E-14* went in
on his third trip July 21st. After a busy week in the
east end of the Marmora he returned westward to
meet Nasmith in *E-11*. On his way up on August
5th the latter found the new net defenses at Nagara
greatly strengthened, and managed to sink a transport carrying troops and supplies to the north
shore.

On the afternoon of the 6th, the two boats met.
Nasmith brought with him the orders for assisting
in the grand attack. The two submarines were to
watch the road used by Turkish troops to reach
the front. At two places it could be seen from the
sea—at Bulair, a place near Gallipoli at the western end of the Marmora, and at the Dohan Aslan
Bank a few miles to the eastward.

The boats were still on the surface exchanging
news when smoke was sighted on the horizon.

Slipping their lines, they set off together to investigate, and found the stranger an enemy gunboat. After an hour and a half's chase *E-11* dived, and *E-14,* acting as a decoy, drew the Turk within easy range of her hidden consort. A well-placed torpedo still further reduced the fast-dwindling Turkish Navy. With the gunboat beached, the two boats came alongside and continued their interrupted conversation.

Before dawn next morning the two boats were submerged at their billets in the straits. Off Bulair, and five miles eastward, the silver finger of a periscope rose above the surface. Eyes fast to rubber eyepieces, two officers eagerly scanned the country for the tell-tale dust of moving troops. Throughout the morning they watched patiently. Three times in *E-14* patience gave way to excitement. Three times she came to the surface prepared to open fire and found her quarry not troops but bullocks.

Commander Boyle was the senior officer, but Commander Nasmith drew the better position. About eleven-thirty he told his anxiously waiting crew that he could see soldiers moving along the road toward Gallipoli. A supply of twelve-pounder shells was placed handy for the gun crew. A quiet order, and *E-11* was brought to the surface. Hatches flew open. The gun layer adjusted his sights to the range already established by cross bearings through the periscope. The breech block was slammed home, and the first shell whined on its way.

With binoculars to his eyes, Nasmith waited tensely for the first burst. It was as nearly perfect as could be. To the marching troops who fancied themselves secure it must have seemed a bolt from the blue. Before they had time to recover from their surprise Nasmith gave the order "Independent fire!" Within a minute a dozen shells sped to their objective. Some were perfect hits; all were disconcerting. The troops scattered. *E-11* modestly hid herself beneath the waters of the Dardanelles.

Half an hour later another column was seen making for the spot on which her gun was ranged. Bobbing to the surface again, she opened fire at once. This time there was no need for a ranging shot, and she got off a dozen rounds rapid fire. The accurate shooting forced the troops to take cover "in open order."

An hour later *E-14's* disappointed crew were roused from their noonday meal by the sharp command, "Surface stations!" Boyle had sighted dust, then the head of a fast-marching column. Probably, from the interval, they were the same soldiery that Nasmith had previously disturbed. *E-14* opened fire with the only thing she had—a six-pounder. The range was such that to reach the target Boyle was forced to lay his gun at its extreme elevation and aim at the top of the hill behind his target. Shortly after he opened fire he heard *E-11* banging away beside him with her twelve-pounder. Nasmith, suspicious of the dispersion of his troops, had followed them along the road.

The two boats conducted a joint shelling for a good hour. *E-14* got off more than forty rounds with her toy gun, and in spite of the long range Boyle spotted six bursts among the infantry, and one shell landed fair in a large building where many had taken cover. *E-11,* with her larger gun, did more serious damage. Through their binoculars both officers saw dead and wounded strewn along the road where the twelve-pounder shells had burst.

The enjoyable gunnery practice was interrupted by the arrival of a field gun. The boat continued shelling until the gun found the range, when its accurate shooting forced both boats to dive. Satisfied that their artillery had driven the impudent submarines away, the column reformed and resumed its march. Promptly the two black hulls bobbed above the surface, the gun crews leaped to their stations, and more profitable shooting was accomplished before the field gun could again be brought to bear.

Next day Commander Boyle ordered Nasmith to change billets with him because his smaller gun would be more effective in the position *E-11* had fought from the previous day. Nasmith had taken up his position before dawn and was watching the road. About four-thirty a searching swing of the periscope showed a battleship steaming westward. She was the *Barbarousse Haireddine,* Turkey's last major fighting ship, and the first battleship to appear outside the Bosphorus in more than two months. She was carrying emergency ammunition to the badly depleted stores on the peninsula. Fussing along with her was a destroyer.

Avoiding the destroyer, Nasmith manœuvred into position on the starboard side of the *Barbarousse Haireddine,* and torpedoed her amidships without permitting the enemy to see his periscope. With the explosion, the battleship listed heavily, and made for the shore. To make certain of her damage, Nasmith invited trouble by exposing his periscope. The wounded Turk accepted the invitation, and opened rapid fire. But his shooting was not good, and Nasmith remained until he saw an explosion in the battleship's fore part. Within twenty minutes of the firing of the torpedo she rolled over and sank.

Neither boat had further opportunity of molesting troops making for the front. After the lesson of the previous day the Turks had brought in field artillery to protect the roads. But as *E-11* found compensation in a battleship, *E-14* bagged a 5,000-ton transport approaching his billet. The trooper beached herself, Boyle told Nasmith what he had found, and together the two boats shelled the transport till she burst into flames.

A few days later Boyle took *E-14* back to her

base. She had seen sixty-eight days, all told, in the
Sea of Marmora, and had done 12,000 miles without an overhaul. Credit for this astounding
achievement was given by Commander Boyle to
his chief engine-room artificer, James Hollier
Hague.

(3)

Left to himself, the pioneer raider of the Marmora found his hunting ground pretty well de-
nuded. A good part of the Turkish Navy was on
the bottom, troop strafing was in the discard, and
nothing roamed the open but hospital ships bearing the wounded of Gallipoli to the hospitals of
Constantinople. Cochrane in *E-7* had found the
same conditions. Nasmith could do nothing but
follow his example. He made for the Gulf of
Ismid where the Kaiser's dream railroad met the
sea.

At Haider Pasha, across from Constantinople,
he crept into the harbour and sunk a large collier
unloading at the pier. It was an important kill, for
coal was not easily come by in Asia Minor. Next he
moved on up the gulf to pay his respects to the viaduct on the Berlin-to-Bagdad railroad that had
already aroused Cochrane's interest.

Between four and five o'clock on the morning
of the 16th *E-11* appeared on the surface and succeeded in getting in fifteen rounds before being
forced under by a rain of fire from the forts on

shore. At six-thirty she sighted a sailing vessel proceeding toward the harbour she had just left. Coming to the surface for a leisurely demolition, she was again forced under by shelling from the shores. Submerging, she proceeded out to sea to get out of range of the shore batteries. Up on the surface again, she was visited by a hostile airplane. Nasmith trimmed the boat down until only her conning tower showed, and remained half out of the open hatch to discover the flier's intentions. When he saw the airplane dropping altitude he waved it good-bye and submerged. He was forty feet down when the first bombs hit the water.

These experiences, while of interest at the moment, were of little value save to confirm the knowledge that conditions in the Marmora had altered vastly since Nasmith first brought *E-11* up in May. For the first time Nasmith and his crew knew a feeling of frustration. Their plight was not unlike that of Alexander when he paused with no more worlds to conquer. Their natural prey had virtually disappeared, thanks to their own insatiable daring. Left them was the apparently unobtainable—a viaduct, an important link in the rail communications which they could affect but trivially with their twelve-pounder gun.

The tactics for its destruction were the source of much discussion between Nasmith, D'Oyly Hughes, and the pilot. When they withdrew to Kalolimni for their weekly wash they devised fan-

tastically hopeful schemes. When *E-2* met them
they were still planning without success. And then
Lieutenant D'Oyly Hughes evolved a plan which
involved great risks and required unusually cool
courage, but which had in its favour some chance
of success.

The more he thought over his plan, the more
convinced he became that he could carry it out successfully. Would Nasmith let him try? That was
the question. Submarine officers were none too
plentiful. The first lieutenant was the most important member of the crew. He was responsible
for the mechanical efficiency of the boat, which
meant that he was responsible for everything.
What attitude would Nasmith take when he
broached the subject of his scheme? Would he
agree or would he consider the risk too great?
Would he decide that Hughes was more valuable
than the destruction of the viaduct? Hughes hoped
not.

As I remember him at Harwich, D'Oyly
Hughes was a tall, cool, handsome chap, very able,
very efficient, and very sure of himself. He was one
of those Britishers to whom the navy was something of an art as well as a profession.

His scheme, briefly, was that *E-11* should go in
as close as possible to the shore, and that he should
swim thence with a sack of gun cotton, land, walk
over to the viaduct, blow it up, and return to *E-11*.
As Hughes told it, it must have sounded very sim-

ple. Nasmith demurred at first but his resistance
was overcome at last by the combined pressure of
his two junior officers. He acceded to the plan
upon one condition. That was that Hughes should
not run any unnecessary risks. Hughes cheerfully
agreed.

The three officers then busied themselves working out every detail of the plan. It was decided to
land the demolition charge and other parapher-
nalia on a small raft. The raft was to be constructed of small empty casks with boards lashed
to the sides and across the tops. Hughes' equipment was to consist of sixteen and one half pounds
of gun cotton, his clothes, a revolver, a sharpened
bayonet (for the silent dispatch of unsuspecting
sentries), an electric torch, and a whistle. The latter for signalling between himself and the boat.
The time chosen for the attempt was 2 A.M. on the
21st.

The 20th was spent preparing the raft and completing the plans. In the evening *E-11* moved off
for her rendezvous with death. Working on schedule, Nasmith took the boat slowly and silently to
within sixty feet of the shore. At that place the
cliffs were high enough to prevent the conning
tower from being seen by any watcher on the railroad tracks. At 2:10 A.M. D'Oyly Hughes gripped
the hand of each of his brother officers and slipped
silently into the water.

Pushing the raft ahead of him, he swam for the

foot of the cliffs. He felt the raft touch, but found the spot he had reached impossible to scale. Imperturbably, he shoved off and swam farther along the shore. Finally he reached a place that could be climbed, and dragged his raft up on the shingle. He donned his clothes, put his revolver and fuse pistol in his pocket, lashed the bayonet to his side, and shouldering the charge of guncotton clambered up the cliffs. He made the top after a stiff climb, and started inland for the railway line.

Stumbling forward in the dark, he floundered into a farmyard. A flock of roosting chickens promptly set up a deafening racket. Hughes took shelter behind a wall and waited agonizing minutes for the commotion he expected from within the dwelling. None came. After the squawking tumult had died down no other sounds broke the stillness so essential to his success. With new caution he moved again toward the railroad.

Reaching the right of way, he crept up on the road bed, and walked four or five hundred yards between the rails in the direction of the viaduct. Ahead of him he caught faint voices. Moving up toward the sounds, he saw three men sitting by the side of the track talking loudly. He laid his guncotton in the ditch and, crouching there himself, waited, watching them. There seemed little chance of their moving on. Beyond them a short distance was the viaduct, too short a distance to attempt creeping past them.

A detour inland was unavoidable if he was to examine the viaduct in privacy. Leaving the guncotton, he crept away from the tracks. From a distance of three hundred yards he saw the viaduct. He saw at once that no one but a madman would attempt to lay a charge. A fire was burning at one end, a stationary engine was at work, and workmen moved to and fro about their tasks.

Convinced of the hopelessness of approaching near this hive of activity, he returned to the railroad, retrieved his guncotton, and made his way a short distance back to where he recalled a small brick culvert. It proved to be less than one hundred and fifty yards from the three men he had found talking. Working with deliberate haste, he dug a hole with the point of his bayonet, and stamped the charge into place. The job completed, he paused for a few minutes, hoping the men would move. They seemed set for the night. While he waited he muffled his fuse pistol as best he could with articles of clothing and then fired it.

The report shattered the stillness of the night. Hughes saw the three Turks jump up and run toward him. Further caution valueless, he fired a couple of shots with his revolver at the running figures. His shots had no effect. Hughes took to his heels, but not in the direction one would expect. Instead of making for the cliffs, he led the three men down the line for about a mile, and then headed for the sea. He knew if he had attempted

to climb down the cliffs where he had landed the
soldiers would have shot him. He decided to lead
them a chase. His enemies were still panting on
behind him when he plunged headlong into the
water about three quarters of a mile from the little cove in which *E-11* was waiting for him. He
did not pause to shed his clothing, so near were his
pursuers. As he swam from the shore he was sorely
disappointed. He had expected to hear the explosion of the charge long before. But suddenly the
ominous rumble of a distant blast reverberated
among the hills, and a few minutes later débris
fell into the water near him. There was no doubt
that his foray had been successful.

He swam off shore for a quarter of a mile. Resting on his back, he blew a long blast on his whistle.
The signal was not heard aboard the submarine.
Hughes waited a little, and turning, swam slowly
back to land. He reached it nearly exhausted, and
pulled himself ashore to rest before discarding
some of his clothing and taking to the water again.

Day was beginning to break when he waded out
again and began his swim toward the boat. At intervals he stopped swimming to rest and blow his
whistle. In turn he let go the bayonet, the revolver,
and the flashlight. It was now fairly light, and he
heard rifle fire on the top of the cliffs which he
knew must be directed at the boat. With the first
shots, the boat heard his whistle signal and backed
slowly out of her bay.

But Hughes, laboriously swimming, did not see
her. What he saw through the dawn mist were
three small rowboats moving slowly in his direction. Certain that any boat in that vicinity would
contain enemies, Hughes swam ashore. There he
hid himself under the rocks and waited for the
three rowboats to move on. Peeping from his hiding place to see what they were doing, he was
astounded to find that they had disappeared. In
their place was *E-11* waiting patiently for his return. What he had actually seen while in the water
was the gun, the bow, and the conning tower.
Through the mist he had mistaken his means of
rescue for a source of danger. Hughes jumped to
his feet, shouted at the top of his voice, and dived
into the water. On board his hail was heard. The
boat came in and he was picked up forty yards off
shore.

The marvel is that he had the stamina to accom-
plish such a feat. Apart altogether from the cool
nerve shown, a climb of sixty feet up precipitous
cliffs, a mile sprint, and a mile swim in clothing
require superb physical condition. And yet
Hughes, it must be remembered, had been cooped
up inside a submarine, with little chance for exercise, and under conditions far from beneficial to
one's health.

In *E-11's* log Nasmith closed the incident with
the same unconcern as he noted his arrival in Constantinople. The entry reads: "5:5 A.M. Dived out

of rifle fire, and proceeded out of the Gulf of
Ismid."

Hughes' splendid exploit seemed to key *E-11*
to new heights of brilliance. On August 22d she
had a stand-up fight with three armed tugs, a destroyer, and a dhow, sank the dhow and one tug,
and captured a bank manager bound for Chanak.
On the 25th she torpedoed two large transports.
On the 28th, she joined *E-2* and shelled the railway yards at Mudania. And just before leaving,
Nasmith went back to the viaduct and used up
most of his remaining ammunition shelling it.

CHAPTER FIVE

I F THE record of British submarines in the Sea of
Marmora was one of unbroken success one might
assume that their difficulties had been exaggerated.
But the achievements of the boats surviving is
made more brilliant by the story of those lost.

I have already referred to the loss of *E-15*.
Early in the campaign she ran aground near the
Kephez mine field inside the entrance to the Dardanelles and was later destroyed by an expedition
in two picket boats from the battleships *Majestic*
and *Triumph*. A short time later the Australian
boat, *AE-2*, was caught by the fire of shore batteries inside the Marmora, and was sunk to prevent her falling into the hands of the enemy.

On September 5th *E-7*, under command of Lieu-

tenant Commander Cochrane, was making her way
up the straits to relieve *E-11* when she ran foul of
the obstructions. These had recently been strengthened, particularly at Nagara. Here there was one
net of wire rope with twelve-foot meshes which
reached to the bottom of the channel. It was
watched by armed patrol boats carrying bombs
and commanded by three batteries on the shore.

Cochrane was fouled by this giant fish trap at
seven-thirty in the morning. After a number of
futile attempts to charge through it, he dived to a
depth of one hundred feet and tried to wriggle
under. He did manage to force his bow through
and used the full power of his motors to complete
the job. The boat strained forward, and it seemed
as if the plunge had gained her freedom, when
one of the propellers was fouled by the obstruction and burned out that motor.

Cochrane then tried to work free with the remaining propeller. With but one propeller moving, and held firmly to the entanglements by the
other, the boat swung broadside to the net and became more hopelessly caught than ever. For more
than eleven hours Cochrane struggled to release
his boat. He tried every trick his long experience
in the deeps had taught him. None bettered his
predicament. If anything, it seemed to grow worse.

On the surface, the buoys holding the net moved
with the struggles of the boat caught below. The
erratic pitching told the restless patrols that they

had at last caught something. They stood by to
watch. A strange game of cat and mouse ensued.
This was before the days of real depth charges, and
a choppy sea was running. To make a kill they had
to lower their bomb or charge on a line. All
through the morning the game was played. On the
surface, Turks watched with confident patience the
heaving of the tell-tale buoys; one hundred feet
below the trapped crew worked obstinately, hoping "by guess or by God" to sever the wires im-
prisoning them.

In the afternoon the sea calmed down a little and
the Turks dropped small mines overboard. Below
in the steel shell, they heard the explosions but
they did not mind them. If I remember rightly,
Cochrane wrote a report on the matter saying:
"We thought it likely that the explosions might
cut the wires holding us, and allow us to proceed."
Toward the middle of the afternoon he ordered
those of the crew not on duty to lie down and have
a rest. Above on the surface the sea grew calmer.

Toward sunset a small boat set out to fish for
the catch. A plumb line felt the bottom for an un-
charted shallow. When it was found a charge of
extra weight was lowered and exploded against the
side of the boat. Inside her all felt a violent shock.
The lights went out, and a hasty examination
showed much of her important mechanism useless.

After one more futile effort, Cochrane, in order
to give his men a chance for their lives, decided to

try to make the surface and surrender. Before making the attempt, the three officers destroyed all confidential papers and methodically carried out arrangements for blowing up the boat before the enemy could get control of her. The charges were laid so that they would not only sink the boat but would also explode the torpedoes. Cochrane believed that these in turn might destroy the net and so enable the boats which were to follow to make the passage where he had failed.

When he was satisfied that he had taken care of every detail, the tanks were blown and *E-7* rose to the surface. As soon as her conning tower broke water gunboats opened fire. When the hatches opened the fire ceased. The last man out was the commander. He and his crew were taken prisoners but the boat was destroyed. Both officers and men were taken to Constantinople, where they were placed in a common jail. Cochrane, in company with Lieutenant Commander Stoker of the Australian boat *AE-2,* made one unsuccessful effort to escape and was captured, but, persisting, he succeeded finally, in 1918, in making his way back to England.

(2)

Very different from this episode was the loss of *E-20*. Late in October Lieutenant Commander Warren took his boat up to relieve *E-12*. It was the practice of boats operating in the Marmora to meet at stated intervals and exchange news of their patrol areas. In this way wasteful duplication of effort was avoided. On October 20th the French submarine *Turquoise* made the passage up the straits and entered the Sea of Marmora, where she met *E-20*. A rendezvous was agreed upon near Rodosto for a later date.

For some reason never very satisfactorily explained, the French boat ran ashore right under the guns of a Turkish fort. She surrendered without destroying any of the confidential documents aboard her. The captured submarine was taken to Constantinople to the natural delight of the local population. In Constantinople at the time was the German submarine *UB-15*. The *Turquoise's* papers were turned over to the German commander. Her rendezvous with *E-20* was discovered. The German kept the appointment.

E-20 waited patiently for her French comrade at the appointed place. Oblivious of her danger, she fell an easy victim to a well-aimed torpedo from *UB-15*. Lieutenant Commander Warren and eight of her crew were saved. The loss of this boat and the *Turquoise* was a distinct blow to the Allied operations in the Sea of Marmora. It left a first-class submarine in the hands of the enemy, and only one boat on patrol. Fortunately, perhaps, that boat was *E-11* under the indomitable Nasmith. Single-handed he kept up his harassing of the enemy. For nearly two months he remained alone on patrol until some other boat could be refitted and sent up to relieve him. In that time he destroyed forty-six enemy ships. Two weeks before his departure Commander Stocks brought in *E-2* again and stayed in with her until recalled on January 2d. On her way down she found the nets gone or demolished. With the abandonment of the Dardanelles campaign no more boats went in.

During the time our boats had been working in the Sea of Marmora they had sunk all the battleships the Turks possessed, five of their gunboats, one destroyer, nine transports, more than thirty steamers, seven ammunition and stores ships, and 188 sailing ships. In the campaign our boats accomplished their purpose. They severed Turkish communications by sea and, in the course of their operations, cost not one noncombatant his life.

Courtesy of the Imperial War Museum

THE U-BOAT FLEET AFTER ITS SURRENDER
Germany had nearly four hundred submarines built
or building when the war ended. None was at sea.
She had neither officers nor crews who would man
them.

Courtesy of the Imperial War Museum

A DEPTH CHARGE EXPLODING
Undersea warfare had no more terrifying weapon
than the depth bomb.

CHAPTER SIX

WHEN Columbus set forth into the West and Scott ventured into the vast unknown of the Antarctic, neither man faced a more uncertain journey than did the crews of the three British submarines, *E-1, E-9,* and *E-11,* when they left their base at Harwich on October 15, 1914, with orders to make their way into the Baltic. Based there on a Russian port, they were to find and attack German warships. As was the case in the Sea of Marmora, to fight the enemy the Trade had first to find him, and to find him our boats had to pass through narrowly guarded waters.

It may seem astonishing to the general reader that the British Fleet was caught napping at the outbreak of war. There was not a single base on

the east coast of Britain protected against attack
by enemy submarines. During the first three
months of the war the mighty Grand Fleet had to
be kept at sea because there was no place in which
it could safely anchor. It dared not stop. The fighting squadrons would rush into Scapa Flow, Loch
Ewe, and Lough Swilly, fuel, and rush out again.
To be on the open sea, protected by a screen of destroyers, was considered safer than any anchorage
on the east coast.

Cromarty was the first harbour to be efficiently
protected against enemy submarines. Once it was,
the battle cruisers under Admiral Beatty were stationed there. The Grand Fleet proper kept dodging from pillar to post up and down the west coast
of Scotland. The enemy knew of the situation.
They sent the *Berlin* to mine the waters about Tory
Island near Lough Swilly, and succeeded in sinking the *Audacious,* one of Britain's latest battleships.

What was more likely than for the enemy to
come out in strength, attack the channel ports and
disrupt the transportation of troops to France,
while our fleet was discreetly keeping out of the
way of German submarines far to the north and
west? These possibilities and many others were
discussed at a naval conference at Loch Ewe held
while the Grand Fleet was fueling. Information
had been received from the intelligence service
that some such sortie was planned by Germany.

It was this information that decided Admiral Jellicoe to send three E-boats into the Baltic. If they could intercept the enemy fleet and attack it as it made its way out of the Baltic there was no knowing just what havoc they might wreak on giant fighting ships caught in narrow waters. Success rested entirely on the chance of making the Baltic unobserved.

It was no easy task. Even peace-time navigation of these waters is so dangerous that this was the most plausible reason put forth by Germany in support of her plan to build the Kiel Canal.

The crews of the three E-boats had not only to face these natural dangers of navigation but a host of others forced on them by the urgent need of secrecy. They had to proceed submerged most of the time. They could rise to charge their batteries only during the darkest hours of the night. The subsurface sets and drifts of currents were unknown to them. Fresh-water rivers emptying into the sea from the Scandinavian shores caused greatly varying densities of water and made diving often a matter of anxious guesswork. On numerous occasions I patrolled these waters myself in *G-6,* and only a person who has done so can have any appreciation of the number or the nature of difficulties.

After the boats had crept cautiously around the Skaw, dodged traffic in the Skagerrak and Kattegat, they had to wait their chance to slip through the Sound during night time. The waters there are very shallow. Proceeding submerged, a submarine would not have sufficient water above her to float a surface vessel. Proceeding at periscope depth, no degree of caution would prevent the eye from being seen.

And there was the weather. Any story of the North Sea that leaves out the weather ignores its most important character. The conning tower of a submarine is not like the navigating bridge of a liner. It is more like a shipwrecked bulkhead. It is crowded for space; there is no chart table, no compass with which to take bearings. The navigator jumps up and down from control room to conning tower like a nervous Jack-in-the-box. He shifts from the bright light of the control room to the blackness above. Blinding sleet and snowstorms, fog and heavy rains drive across his straining sight.

In the Sound there is always heavy traffic between Denmark and Sweden. The sea way is like a busy harbour. The navigator stares at the baffling conglomeration of lights around him, and tries to pick out those that will aid him in navigation. There are hundreds of shore lights, lights on passing vessels, strange signal lights on patrol boats, special lights on fishing craft busy at their trade. Lights everywhere except on the dark, sinister shape sneaking along, trimmed down close to the water, ready to plunge to the bottom with the first note of the Klaxon. The fingers of the officer on watch never wander far from the little button that makes the signal for a crash dive ring through the boat. Without warning, the multitude of lights are wiped out of the navigator's sight. A passing rainstorm or a bank of fog envelops everything in a gray blanket, and the surrounding dangers become a thousand times more trying by their invisibility.

One of the officers who made that trip used to tell a story when asked what it was like. He was on watch and passed down an order through the voice pipe to the helmsman at the lower steering position. The order was misunderstood. The submarine's head began to fall off the opposite way to that required. The officer grew acrimonious, and with reason. They had passed, by uncomfortably few feet, a patrol boat steaming without lights. The sailor offered an explanation, and was brusquely told to go to hell. His voice, weighted with grave courtesy, came up the pipe: "Do you think I would be here, sir, if I knew the way?"

(2)

The officers and men who manned *E-1, E-9,* and *E-11* were probably the most experienced submarine operators in the world. Years of peace-time training had schooled them in all the risks peculiar to this branch of the service. Unlike the German Admiralty, which did not realize the effectiveness of the submarine until after war had actually begun, the British had been developing the mechanical killer-whales since 1904, when, unescorted, a flotilla of A-boats engaged in fleet manœuvres.

The three commanders, N. F. Laurence, Max. E. Horton and Martin E. Nasmith, were all young men. There is no need to tell again what manner of man Nasmith was. The story of his exploits in the Dardanelles has already accomplished any characterization possible. All three, early in the war, had won the admiration and, to a large extent, the envy of the entire service for their courage and accomplishments on patrols in the North Sea.

Horton had made three adventurous patrols by October, 1914. The first of these was within a few hours of the declaration of war when he took his boat into Heligoland Bight where he sat on the bottom playing bridge and praying for the sight of an enemy fighting ship. The second patrol took him to the same place later in August with no better hunting luck.

On September 12th *E-9* was on her third patrol off Germany's front dooryard. She rested all night in 120 feet of water and all hands had a comfortable night's rest. With the first flick of dawn she rose slowly to the surface of a still sea fogged with light dawn mists. Her position was only six miles S. S. W. of the harbour of Heligoland. As the boat steadied to the proper depth for a diving patrol Horton raised periscope. He watched. The mist was thinning. Through its weak tatters he thought he caught a shape. The fog cleared and showed him an enemy light cruiser about two miles away.

Horton was able to get within six hundred yards of her when he recognized her as the light cruiser *Hela*. He told the crew. Nerves tightened, eyes steadied, breathing became a conscious effort. It was a great moment. Our men were still smarting under the loss of H. M. S. *Pathfinder*. And at last the enemy had been found. Here was the chance to even the score.

The crew stood silently at their action stations. Their eyes were glued on the youthful commander crouching with his hands on the handles of the periscope gear. He watched the seconds tick off the interval until he should show the periscope for the clipped second needed to fire a torpedo.

The motors had stopped. All machinery was silent save for the whirr of the hydroplane wheels or the steering wheel. The tension was great. The atmosphere was charged like a mine. Horton glanced at the clock, the depth gauge, and the compass. "Raise periscope!" Crouching almost to his knees, he raised himself with it, his eye glued to the rubber eyepiece. The moment daylight penetrated the lense he shouted, "Stop periscope!" True to his calculations, the *Hela* was steaming past, oblivious of the menace lurking on her beam.

"Fire one . . . fire two!" The order rang through the compartment like the crack of a revolver. There was a hiss and a muffled roar followed by a slight shock as the torpedoes left the tubes. Then all waited for the explosion. *E-9* dived the second the torpedoes left on their death journey. Horton was taking no chances of alarming the enemy before his last moment. As *E-9* dived the explosion occurred.

E-9 was brought up to periscope depth again. The force of the explosion had stopped the *Hela* dead in her tracks. She took a heavy list to starboard. Horton was studying the success of his attack, when suddenly he was made aware of his own danger. A salvo of shells splattered around the periscope. They came from ships he had not seen. Again *E-9* dived, but only for a moment.

Evading the attentions of a swarm of mosquito craft, Horton raised periscope again, determined to see the death like a hunter who tracks his kill that he may deliver the last needed shot. But there was no need. The cruiser had gone. All Horton saw was a number of armed trawlers rescuing men on the spot where she had gone down.

Then started forty-eight hours of a living inferno for the crew of the British submarine. A nest of enemy destroyers circled her position and hunted her all day. The water was not deep enough for safety. Several times *E-9* narrowly escaped ramming. Countless times her hull was brushed by the slowly searching tendrils of sweeps. When darkness came the batteries were dangerously low. All that night *E-9* and the surface craft played hide and seek in deadly earnestness. Time after time the submarine rose to the surface to get her charge under way and was sent into a crash dive by the onrushing rams of the destroyers. Under these conditions the batteries were partly charged.

Next day the weather sided with the enemy. A full gale lashed the shallow waters into a fury of flying foam and breaking wave tops. The short steep seas made it impossible for *E-9* to keep her trim at periscope depth. The pumping made it impossible for her to stay on the bottom. The enemy and the high seas made it seem almost impossible for her to proceed on the surface. In spite of these difficulties, her men managed to bring her back safely to Harwich with word that they had avenged the *Pathfinder*.

On his next patrol Horton bagged another. October 6th saw *E-9* completing a long siege at the mouth of the River Ems—a disappointing, vexatious, harassing patrol; the kind of patrol that the Trade was to know in wearisome repetition throughout the war. Horton had expected surely to sight big game in those days when the true modesty of the enemy was as yet unknown. The crew was keyed up, anxious to avenge the loss of the *Aboukir, Cressy,* and *Hogue,* which had fallen victims to the German submarine *U-9*.

U-9's achievement will always stand out prominently in naval history. Weddigen, her commander, was terribly handicapped. His boat was old and far from reliable, and his sinking of the three British cruisers in quick succession made the world realize for the first time the ferocious menace of the submarine. It must also be admitted that the measure of the German success was due, to a great extent, to the early policy of heroic but useless sacrifice followed by the British crews, each of which in turn stood by to pick up the survivors of the earlier sinking. It was a policy, incidentally, which was never followed again in the war.

During his patrol Horton had set his torpedoes to run deep enough to disable and sink deep-draughted warships. He had nosed in and around narrow channels and shallow waters infested by enemy patrols. *E-9* dodged small craft, slid from under the prows of destroyers, and night after night, more by good luck than by anything else, had managed while on the surface to charge her batteries for the following day's work. Only by gifted skill and daring had Horton kept his presence in the Ems a secret. Hour after hour the officers had strained their eyes at the periscope for sight of cruisers or battleships. During the long patrol none entered or left the harbour.

October 6th was the last possible day they could remain on patrol. The hours of daylight dragged along to final disappointment. Just before turning and heading out to sea Horton ordered his first lieutenant to set two torpedoes to run at shallow depth—about eight feet. This done, he set off to

bag one of the destroyers which had helped make
the patrol a continuous nightmare. It was no easy
ambition. The destroyer Horton picked kept altering her course. The batteries were low. Vast quantities of juice are drained chasing at full speed to
head off a coy victim who changes course every
few minutes.

I knew Max Horton well during the time we
served together in the Blyth flotilla. I can imagine
his language as he was thwarted in his attack time
after time. He was an inveterate cigarette smoker,
and must have wanted a fag desperately, but it was
impossible to smoke in air you could almost cut
with a knife.

With the batteries run down the attack looked
hopeless and Horton was on the point of heading
for home when the destroyer again unreasonably
altered course and headed straight for *E-9*,
trimmed just below the surface. *E-9* had to speed
up again, this time to get out of the way and to increase the range. As the enemy destroyer *S-116*
dashed past, Horton gave the command to fire. The
torpedo ran true. It crashed home amidships, and
with a tremendous explosion the stricken scout slid
below the surface. *E-9* headed for home.

This was one of the boats chosen for the Baltic
patrols. From the outbreak of hostilities the crew
had been almost continuously in enemy waters, but
they were no sooner back in Harwich than they
were ordered to get the boat ready for sea and to

put out on one of the most dangerous expeditions of the war.

Lieutenant Commander Laurence was much the same type of officer as Horton. He had done the same patrols but without the same success, due entirely to a lack of opportunities. Nasmith, the reader already knows, and nothing can gauge the difficulties of the Baltic adventure better than to admit that they defeated the crew of *E-11* and forced Nasmith to turn back to Harwich. The failure was nothing to his discredit. Nasmith and his men proved their skill and courage often enough in the Dardanelles and the Sea of Marmora. There Nasmith was awarded the Victoria Cross, "For Valour," yet Horton and Laurence succeeded in the North Sea where Nasmith failed, not through any fault of his own or his crew's but because every card seemed stacked against them. He got all the bad breaks and none of the good.

(3)

E-9 and *E-1* arrived safely in the Baltic on October 18, 1914. In a later chapter the passage through the entrance is described in detail and it would be pointless to repeat it here. Both boats passed through by guess, by the grace of God, and by luck. Their orders were to proceed to Danzig, from which port the German High Seas Fleet was known to be operating.

Long before reaching there Laurence had his first brush with the enemy. He fell in with the light cruiser *Victoria Luise* when in a most uneasy position for an attack. The water was shallow. When the boat was on the bottom there was less than fifteen feet over the conning tower. Laurence accepted the risks, fired his bow torpedoes, and went to the bottom. The breathless interval followed when the crew waited tensely for the explosion. None came. One torpedo ran deep and passed under the cruiser. Seeing the wake of the first tin fish, the *Victoria Luise* lost no time putting her helm hard over and was lucky enough to see the racing tube of death skim across her bows. Within two hours of this unfruitful attack Laurence met two more enemy cruisers. He chased after them, but owing to their angle on his bow, and their course and speed, he was not able to make an attack. He then proceeded as requisite to Bornholm, a large island in the southern Baltic, with the intention of operating there the next day.

Horton's passage included a merry time with a squadron of destroyers which discovered him in the narrow waters of the island-strewn sea. He extricated himself and toured the coast seeking a likely victim. Laurence paid Danzig a visit, and after diving at great risk right into the harbour of Neufahrwasser had the provoking experience of seeing three enemy cruisers in the basin without being able to attack them. *E-1* hung around like a cat watching a canary's cage, but luck was not with her. It was with the three enemy ships all unconscious of the threat that waited outside their base.

E-1 then found it imperative to reach her Baltic base which was to be the Russian port of Libau. The trip had placed a terrific strain on her mechanical plant. Engines and motors demanded attention. She and her consort, *E-9,* following the instructions received at Harwich, proceeded as requisite to Libau, not knowing that the Russians had abandoned it as a naval base. Unaware of their danger, both boats went right into the harbour through a mine field of great dimensions laid by the German Fleet. When the two boats arrived, after passing safely through rows upon rows of the sea's swiftest death, they discovered the port deserted.

A Russian officer was found who advised them to proceed to Lapvik, but they were more concerned about *E-11* than about themselves. They put back to sea in search of Nasmith's boat, keeping an eye open as well for any enemy craft. Three days' hunting discovered neither *E-11* nor the enemy, save one destroyer that *E-1* fired at and missed. Disgusted, they gave up the hunt, and in compliance with orders received from the British ambassador to Russia, moved north and reported for duty to the commander in chief of the Russian Fleet.

The crews of both boats gave up *E-11* for lost. They were mistaken. Nasmith had run into every conceivable kind of bad luck but he was still afloat. *E-11* had developed engine trouble, her motors had gone wrong, and it was the night of the 20th before she could even attempt the passage through the sound. Unlucky by night, she tried to thread the sea lane by daylight so that she might be in time to help if the German sortie from Danzig materialized.

Going through, Nasmith's periscope was sighted, and he discovered that he was being followed. When he reached the narrow shallow entrance to the sound repeated attempts were made to ram him. The boat escaped her doom several times by the shadow of a hair. Unable to proceed, unable to shake off the enemy, *E-11* was forced to turn back.

Outside the sound a submarine was sighted on the surface. Believing it to be the German boat *U-3*, they fired and fortunately missed, for it turned out to be a Danish boat. The firing of the torpedo disclosed their position, brought another host of troubles and an added strain on the failing batteries. Still Nasmith persevered, and decided to make the attempt again on the following night. During the afternoon he found a quiet stretch of empty sea and rose to the surface to charge batteries. No sooner did the black wedge of the conning tower break water than the boat was sighted by an enemy plane. Shortly afterward the inevitable German destroyers swarmed to the attack and hunted the boat all that night.

Nasmith returned to Harwich hoping that Commander Keyes would allow him to make the attempt again as soon as *E-11* could be put in shape. She was chosen for other work, the important task of crashing the Dardanelles. When the crew heard that they had been picked for the special task in the Near East they were the happiest men in the entire navy. One hard-boiled Jack tried to express how happy they were by saying: "We all felt so blinkin' low about the Baltic show we'd have hunted asbestos battleships with a celluloid submarine in hell, if the commander had asked us to."

E-1 and *E-9* set industriously to work at Lapvik, *E-1* to repair her damaged engines, *E-9* to prowl the cold waters of the Baltic. Patrols were made until it was necessary to have an ice breaker precede the boats in and out of harbour, when the driving spray froze six and eight inches deep on the super-structure.

Some notion of the potency of the submarine, handled by capable crews, is given by the fact that two boats, operating from a not-too-satisfactory base, were able to control shipping in the Baltic just as, later, one or two boats did in the Sea of Marmora. Before they had been long at Lapvik the enemy fleet ceased its attentions to the Russian ports. Enemy warships became almost as scarce in the enclosed waters as they were in the North Sea. As a result the British boats were able to cripple effectively the large traffic in ore and magnetic iron which was going on between Sweden and Germany, and which was the latter's main source of supply for munitions. The thoroughness of the British operations in this work was severely curtailed because our submarine commanders respected the lives of noncombatants, and not a single vessel was sunk without due warning, nor without provision made for the safety of its crew.

CHAPTER SEVEN

IN JANUARY, 1915, Max Horton took *E-9* to sea
on a test trip to discover whether the terrible cold
would make a long journey impossible. An ice
breaker crushed a path out of the harbour for him.
Proceeding on the surface, the boat was soon a
miniature berg encased in glittering ice. One man
had to be kept continuously at work chopping ice
from the combing of the upper hatch so that the
lid could be tightly closed if the boat were forced
into a hurried dive. Horton was anxious to learn
if the slush ice in vents and valves would render
diving impossible or dangerous. Under the surface, however, conditions were found to be normal. The salt water thawed the frozen slush in all

the numerous places essential to the diving efficiency of the boat.

Satisfied that E-9 had the arctic nature of a polar bear, Horton set out for the sound, proceeding as requisite to avoid enemy mine fields and the annoyances of small patrol boats. In the middle of that afternoon he sighted an enemy destroyer about six hundred yards off. She was practically abeam E-9 and offered a good target. A bow tube was flooded and fired. Through the periscope Horton watched the torpedo out of its tube. It appeared to pick up its depth and be running well one hundred yards from the boat. The first few seconds after a tin fish is loosed is an anxious time, particularly if it has been set to swim at shallow depth. It may break surface and give the whole show away. When it does, it may develop a failure in the gyroscopic steering control. Then it will run around in circles like a dog chasing its tail. It was always a temptation to watch how one was going to act.

Satisfied that this one was behaving, Horton took a last quick glance at the destroyer and lowered periscope. Then came the anxious wait. Every man aboard silently counted forty-five seconds, the time it would take the torpedo to reach its mark. Forty-five seconds passed. No explosion. The men relaxed glumly, satisfied the shot had missed. At fifty seconds there came a dull heavy boom and the concussion threw some of the men off their feet. Horton raised periscope. Four minutes from the time the torpedo sped away from the tube the destroyer had disappeared completely!

During the night *E-9* came to the surface to charge her batteries. The night was viciously cold. Overhead the stars stabbed back and forth in the sky. The sharp wash covered the boat with ice. The officer and lookout slowly froze, unable to move energetically enough to keep up circulation. Another man with an axe and sharpened scraper kept the hatch combing clear of ice. Below numbed men went about their duties. The leading torpedo ratings kept on with the work of charging the precious batteries. Some tried to sleep, muffled up in their white woollen running gear, duffle bags, and sweaters. By midnight the boat was so coated with ice that Horton took her to the bottom and rested there until she thawed out.

Under such conditions the crews of *E-1* and *E-9* worked during the winter of 1914–15. Added to the difficulties imposed by Nature and by the inherent villainy of a submarine's temperament, they were working among strangers whose language they did not understand and whose habits were entirely foreign to them.

With the opening of navigation, patrols began again in earnest. Sometimes working in pairs, sometimes singly, our boats contrived to control between them the sea ways of the Baltic, and to contribute, very materially, in dissuading Germany from prosecuting an ambitious scheme to attack Petrograd. The war, as far as Russia was concerned, was now entering its most critical phase, and but for the activities of the two British boats the German armies might possibly have finished the summer in Petrograd.

Early in July *E-9* escaped by inches the ram of an enemy destroyer. In his log Horton ignored the manner of this happening to note another matter. "We had just time to see another large vessel about five miles away before dipping." Ignoring the destroyer, he set off after the bigger game, but lost her. Provoked, he brought *E-9* up and continued the patrol on the surface where there was a better view to be had than through the canned eye. At 7 P.M. the officer on watch reported smoke to the northward.

In those northern latitudes there was still light enough to execute an attack. Horton submerged and steered to head off the approaching vessel. After an anxious wait a cautious peep through the periscope showed the smoke to be an enemy light-cruiser squadron of two *Auburg* type vessels, a four-funnelled cruiser and an escort of destroyers.

E-9 was in a most delicate position. There was not enough water under her for comfort. Once her presence was made known, the destroyers were certain to acknowledge it. He could have chanced a long shot but this did not appeal to Horton: finding a German squadron in the open was too rare a chance to be thrown away through excess caution.

The enemy ships were proceeding at full speed, the destroyers like busy dragon flies on their flanks. Throwing caution to the winds, Horton attacked at full speed, diving under the destroyers and coming up at periscope depth between them and their charges. Opposite *E-9* was the rear ship of the line, the largest of the lot. In the seconds at his disposal Horton estimated the enemy's speed, the necessary deflection, the range, and let loose the racing mines. Thanks to his brilliant marksmanship, the *Prinz Adalbert* was seriously damaged and was out of commission for some weeks.

E-1 under Commander N. F. Laurence was far from inactive. By this time he had several transports and ore ships to his credit and had picked off a German mine layer from under the nose of her escorting destroyers. Then came a period of hard luck when she was forced into port for repairs and *E-9* carried on alone.

Back on the job in August, hard luck again robbed Laurence of one of the most important kills of the entire war. One morning, when the watches were changing and those relieved were interested in breakfast, the officer on watch sighted a squadron of enemy battle cruisers steaming line abreast. *E-1's* crew leaped from the breakfast table to action stations. In less than ten minutes from the time the enemy was sighted the two bow torpedoes were on their way. The weather conditions were extremely bad. Low visibility, banks of fog, and a

choppy sea worked against the submarine's crew.
Out of the fog bank dashed destroyers. Not one,
or two, but a whole squadron of them.

While diving to avoid these, the crew felt the
concussion of the exploding torpedo. Unable to
raise the periscope for a look, they were forced to
wait until later to learn the result of the shot. Commander Laurence knew that he had fired at one of
the *Moltke* class. As it turned out, it was the
Moltke herself. The torpedo only damaged her
and she was able to limp back to port where she
was repaired in a little more than a month.

The incident had its moral effect. German ships
were withdrawn from the vicinity of Riga, and
their operations abandoned at that point. German
crews were ordered to concentrate on the pair of
E-boats, and were told that the destruction of one
British submarine would be considered of greater
value than the sinking of one of the larger Russian
battleships. The Tsar sent for Commander Laurence and thanked him personally with the words,
"You have saved our town of Riga."

(2)

The effectiveness of the work done by these two
E-boats, the growing dependence of Germany on
Swedish iron ore, and the pressure exerted by the
German Army on the Russian flank resting on the
Baltic were all factors in determining the British
Admiralty to reinforce the Baltic patrols. In doing

so we were only repaying the debt owed Russia from those days when she threw her armies on the eastern front and diverted tens of thousands of trained German troops from the west.

Four C-class boats were sent around to the north of Russia and transported by rivers, railroads, and canals down to the Baltic. There they were assembled and fitted out before they took their places in the patrols that harassed the enemy shipping to the end. Three E-class boats were sent from Harwich, our principal submarine base. They were *E-8, E-13,* and *E-19.* All boats numbered 13 were notoriously unlucky. *K-13* was sunk with all hands while doing her trials. *G-13* was always a Jonah boat, although she did have luck when she sank the German submarine *UC-43* in April, 1917. But the fate that befell *E-13* was the worst of the ill-numbered lot. Her end won the sympathy of the world, and no single incident during the war, with the exception of the death of Edith Cavell, aroused such a storm of indignation against Germany.

Feeling her way through the narrow channels that divide Norway and the coast of Denmark, *E-13* ran aground off Saltholm on the south shore. Owing to the state of the tide, she could not be floated, and stayed high and dry on a sand bar separated from the mainland by a channel some four hundred yards wide. She was ashore on Danish territory. She was helpless to do any harm even had the crew wanted to. According to all the rules of civilized warfare, she was out of the game. According to international law, she had to be interned together with her crew until the end of hostilities if she failed to float herself in twenty-four hours.

All night the crew worked trying to get her off. When dawn came they were sitting around, silent and morose, disgusted at their luck. Lieutenant Commander G. Layton, *E-13's* captain, found it hard to speak to the men who had served with him so faithfully, and whom Fate had rendered inactive till the end of the war.

At 5 A. M. a Danish destroyer arrived. Her officers were very polite. They were profuse in their regrets that *E-13* should have been so unfortunate. They hoped that the British sailors would be more successful in their efforts at the next high tide. But if they were not, the Danes pointed out, the Danish commander would be forced to ask for their surrender and internment as soon as the twenty-four hours allowed by international law had expired. The Danish boat stationed an armed guard to watch proceedings.

The first lieutenant of *E-13* went over to the guard ship to discuss the situation with the senior officer. Almost immediately a German destroyer came on the scene. She stood by, and watched. The next visitors were two Danish torpedo boats, and at 9 A.M. a third one arrived. From the exposed decks of their boat the crew of *E-13* sourly watched the marine conference gather. On the heels of the last Dane two German destroyers were seen coming up out of the south. The leading German steamed to within a thousand yards of the stranded E-boat and hoisted some commercial flag signal. Before there was time to decode the signal the destroyer let loose a torpedo. It struck the bottom below *E-13* and fortunately did no damage. That was to follow.

Completely ignoring the Danish ships, the German then closed to three hundred yards and opened a heavy fire, using all guns that could be brought to bear on the target. In a moment *E-13* was in flames both fore and aft. Wounded men lay writhing in agony on steel decks rapidly heating from the conflagration that raged inside.

His face livid with anger, Lieutenant Commander Layton, issued his last order from the decks of *E-13*. "To the water, men . . . swim for it . . . head for the shore or the Danish ship . . . get away from those damned swine."

And as the men who were unwounded did as they were ordered, the enemy changed the type of shells being used to destroy the submarine and used instead shrapnel and machine-gun fire on the men swimming for their lives. The Danes proved themselves men of big hearts and great courage. The insignificant little torpedo boats steamed boldly between the maniacal destroyer and her helpless victims.

The challenge of the Danes was not accepted. Fire ceased and the German ships withdrew. The Danish crews did everything in their power for our men, but of the thirty-one officers and men who made up *E-13's* complement, fifteen were either killed or wounded.

It seems hard now to understand how such an outrage could have occurred. The reason, it seems to me, was sheer hatred, added to the fear the enemy had of our submarines and their crews. If Horton and Laurence with only two boats had been able to control ship movements in the Baltic, what would be the result when more E-boats joined the patrols?

But if they destroyed his command and killed his men, they only increased the determination of Layton to have vengeance. From the moment he got ashore he worked unremittingly to escape, and it was my good fortune to be present when, after making one of the most spectacular escapes of the war, he walked into the depot ship to greet his brother officers and take command of another submarine.

(3)

Ignorant of the fate which had befallen his consort, Lieutenant Commander Goodhart proceeded as requisite as far as the Skagerrak without any real adventure, but from then on he and *E-8* had their share of it. Goodhart appears to have been about the only British submarine commander who wrote anything of his adventures in detail. During the war there was sent around the Trade a confidential paper describing his passage into the Baltic. Its purpose was to help other boats which might have to do the same thing. Because of its extraordinary interest it is worth repeating here with some condensation.

Having entered the Skagerrak early in the afternoon, *E-8* was forced under to avoid detection by a large fleet of enemy trawlers. She was kept under until 7 P.M. Proceeding on the surface at full speed, Goodhart rounded the Skaw and headed up the Kattegat. The critical part of the adventure now lay ahead. Naturally, *E-8* had to run without lights. Traffic in these waters is always congested, and Goodhart had to move forward with the utmost caution to give all vessels a wide berth.

At three in the morning of August 18th he was obliged to dive to avoid the traffic in the narrow channel. For two and a half hours *E-8* rested on the bottom because the water was too shallow to permit her to move submerged in safety. About 5:30 A.M. the sound of propellers overhead was no longer heard, and Goodhart rose to periscope depth for a cautious look around.

He ventured to the surface only to be forced into a crash dive by a ship he had failed to notice through the tube. Another hour and half went by, and once again he stole up for a look. A fog had settled down and under its cover *E-8* raced at full speed toward the sound.

While the fog might be termed a friendly fog in as much as it offered protection from the lookouts of steamers, it added immeasurably to the anxious strain of the conning-tower watch and the navigating officer. For them fog meant virtual blindness, and theirs was the responsibility of avoiding collision and stranding.

As the sun grew stronger the fog lifted and *E-8* was forced down again just after the crew had finished breakfast. She crept along submerged at about three knots until the early afternoon, when Goodhart was able to take periscope bearings and establish his position as in the entrance to the sound. He had then to decide whether to proceed submerged or wait and make a rush for it in the darkness. Confident of the skill of his navigating officer, he decided to negotiate the narrow channel submerged.

The number of trawlers, ships, and patrol vessels in the sound made it a risky matter to expose the periscope for so much as a few seconds. A glimpse of the canned eye, caught from a passing vessel, would have exposed *E-8's* presence, her position, and her intentions. At the Baltic entrance to the sound German patrol boats would have gathered to welcome her through. Quite apart from the dislike a submarine has for armed surface craft, it was imperative that *E-8* be free to charge her batteries as soon as possible after the long run submerged. Goodhart dived to a depth between fifty and sixty feet and proceeded as requisite.

Until three in the afternoon they crept along guided by the sixth sense submarine navigators acquire. Then came an interval when there was no sound overhead and they rose to twenty feet for a quick look through the periscope. While the commander swept the surface for shipping the navigator was able to get his bearings. Course was altered to take the boat through the northern narrows.

Exactly one hour later another quick glimpse showed that they were right on their course and abreast of Helsingör Light. For an hour and a half they again moved forward submerged and then went to the bottom in eleven fathoms to wait for darkness, well satisfied that they had gone so far without being seen.

(4)

One bell in the first watch found the crew rested and *E-8* on the surface ready for the hardest part of the trip. The Swedish coast was dark and forbidding but to the south Denmark was ablaze with lights. It is almost impossible on a dark night to pick out those lights that are intended for you, or ignore the myriad of others that may lead you to your destruction. That is why surface vessels take

aboard pilots familiar with local conditions. *E-8*
had to proceed alone.

Altering course to the southwestward, she shortly
came upon two destroyers. They were steaming
north along the Danish coast at a fine show of
speed. One of them passed quite close but dashed
on. Then suddenly she turned sixteen points and
stopped. What to do then was a question. Should
they dive? Had they been seen?

On the conning tower, Goodhart and his navigating officer coolly debated the matter. They decided to proceed. The destroyer moved off again
slowly, hesitated, and then stopped. It was evident
that someone aboard her had seen, or thought he
had seen, the ominous shape low in the water.
Next, an officer of the watch had probably investi-
gated and, sighting nothing, had decided his lookout was mistaken. On such little incidents does the
success or failure of a cruise depend. While this
dramatic fragment was being enacted on the
bridge, part of the crew closed up at their stations
and the rest lay down near their posts, reading or
snatching a few moments' sleep.

Next they had to enter the narrow, dangerous
channel that would lead them past Copenhagen.
The lights of the city blazed a bright patch in the
surrounding dark. From the Middle Ground Fort
searchlights swept fingers of cold white light
across the conning tower of the submarine. The
cone of marching light passed and the two officers

stared again into the darker night, watching now a silhouette of black slide between them and the city lights, now staring into the blackness on their port beam. There were breathless moments when they thought of nothing but immediate dangers; there must have been other moments when they thought of how, a century before, Lord Nelson with his old wooden sailing ships had come into these very same waters to give battle to the Danish Fleet in its own harbour.

While their attention was distracted by the beams of the searchlights, *E-8* nearly ran into several fishing craft. The helm had to be put hard over to avoid them. Safely past, they changed course again for Flint Channel.

At ten-thirty they were almost abreast of Malmö on the Swedish coast. The shore line here was brighter than the Danish coast opposite. They had no means of reading their charts on the conning tower. To have shown a light meant suicide. The navigating officer hopped back and forth from the control room, doing his best to advise his commander and to fix the boat's position. About them were dozens of fishing vessels each carrying two or more lights. All had to be avoided.

To be ready for any emergency, Goodhart ordered the boat to be trimmed down until her decks were completely awash and only the conning tower was above water. He also ordered one engine to be disconnected, and proceeded with the other engine at seven knots. In this trim, the boat was ready to dive in a few seconds.

Between twenty and thirty vessels were passed on the way through Flint Channel, and then Goodhart noticed a ship directly ahead using a searchlight. Luckily the beam was trained on the sky as if passing signals to some distant shore station. There was no mistaking the fact that something was wrong. The atmosphere seemed heavy with danger. Many of the vessels dashed about on erratic courses. Were they the cause? Had the earlier searchlights discovered that a submarine was in the sound?

Altering course to avoid some fishing vessels, Goodhart was forced to pass close to a ship at anchor. She first showed a green light and then three white ones. They were not anchor lights. What could they mean? Immediately ahead were two more steamers and the vessel with the sky-flung searchlight. A lightship with her three vertical lights slid by, and as *E-8* passed this aid to navigation she found herself within two hundred yards of a torpedo boat.

A few seconds and there remained no doubt as to the intentions of the warship. Red and green flares sizzled upward from her decks. She changed course to ram the submarine. The chase was on in earnest.

The trim of the boat enabled Goodhart to do a crash dive in time to allow the enemy to pass over her without touching. The commander dropped through the hatch, and before he could properly close the lid of the hatch the boat had bumped on a very hard bottom. A number of the crew were thrown off their feet.

The bump did not worry Goodhart. When he finished securing the lid he found that the depth gauges registered only eighteen feet. A deep draft vessel could still slice the frail skin like a can opener. Hurriedly adjusting her trim, the men got the boat off bottom and tried to proceed. The depth of water lessened to fourteen feet and the conning tower was barely below the surface. Like a fish dropped from a hook *E-8* started to wriggle out of the shallows. A series of heavy bumps and the boat came to a dead stop. It was near midnight. The few remaining hours of darkness were none too many to allow them to reach the comparative security of the Baltic.

Goodhart brought her to the surface. Drogden Light was on the starboard quarter. Less than two hundred and fifty yards ahead was either a large destroyer or a light cruiser. He was plainly trapped. Again he took the boat down as far as he could in the hope that he might creep by unseen if sufficiently close. The plan was successful: *E-8* sneaked under the towering shadow of the destroyer safely, only to find, four minutes later, another destroyer blocking the way one hundred yards ahead.

He dipped to slip under this new danger, and told his first lieutenant to trim her at twenty-three feet. The plan was excellent, but there was not twenty-three feet of water. *E-8* struck bottom heavily on her starboard side. The mad whine of the racing starboard motor told him that she had stripped the blades off that propeller.

E-8, or rather the men within her, could do nothing but sit and listen to the flail of enemy propellers overhead. Not exactly overhead, because had they passed directly over her, their sharp bows would have slit her open. The fingers of the clock in the control room crept slowly on. Eight silvery bells told of the arrival of a new day. Who will wonder if the men, with ears straining for every sound, asked themselves, "Will August 19th see our finish?" When the striking bells were quiet again, a deeper silence emphasized the ticking of the clock.

Under such conditions inaction is maddening. At 12:15 A.M. Goodhart decided to make another attempt to get clear. Pumping sufficient water out of the boat's tanks to ease her off the bottom, he headed for deeper water. A series of bumps and the gauges registered eighteen feet. A few minutes later he told the crew that he would try the surface again.

Adjusting the trim of the boat with great delicacy, so that she could be controlled by the hydroplane gear alone, he gave the order to rise. The boat came to the surface as quietly as a sleeping whale. Goodhart quickly opened the lid of the hatch and poked his head through. As his eyes accustomed themselves to the darkness, the first shape they caught was that of a destroyer close by the starboard beam. The first lieutenant was standing ready under the lower hatch, awaiting the orders of his captain. "Take her down slowly to seventeen feet. Don't hit bottom. And steer your present course." Thus they crept by the enemy, almost scraping her side.

For nearly two hours things went well. At a few minutes after two she struck bottom at eighteen feet. Nothing could be seen through the periscope in the darkness, so Goodhart again went to the surface and opened the conning tower hatch. The destroyer was still on the port bow, but now she was nearly a mile away. Greatly relieved, Goodhart dipped as deep as he dared and proceeded as requisite. At seven-fifteen a quick look found a clear horizon.

This gave a chance to get the charging of the batteries under way. The boat was brought to the surface and continued there until forced to dive around 9 A. M. to escape a steamer. Shortly after she was back on the surface, driving into the east and making precious juice for the cells. At six bells (11 A. M.) she was put under again by an enemy destroyer.

It seemed impossible to charge the batteries during daylight and the lack of juice made it impossible to travel submerged. With power remaining, Goodhart would have attacked the destroyer and got rid of her expeditiously. Without it he was forced to the bottom where he remained in twenty-three fathoms until 6: 40 P. M. All hands needed the sleep, and when *E-8* came again to the surface everyone on board was feeling in good shape. A peep through the periscope and they plunged to bottom again. A Swedish vessel was patrolling ahead of them. As darkness closed down, Goodhart once more started charging, but a patrol of three ships put him under again.

The patrol was moving slowly eastward. An hour later *E-8* came up again, but now the moon was so bright that she was promptly sighted by a destroyer. Under she went with her batteries almost gone, like those of an automobile on a zero morning. The hours dragged on till midnight when at last there were found two free hours in which to make juice. Before diving, the navigator was able to fix the boat's position. Rügen was on the starboard beam and dead ahead was the Island of Bornholm. They were clear of the sound, and once past Bornholm the free expanse of the Baltic lay before them.

At 9 A. M. another chance came to run on the surface, but not for long enough to charge the batteries fully. Goodhart went to the bottom again, planning to slip past Bornholm during darkness and get his charge in as he passed. Everything went according to schedule until 9 : 00 P. M. on the night of August 21st when an enemy light cruiser tried to ram him. By this time the crew of *E-8* was indifferent to such tactics. The reader must remember that the depth charge had not been invented. Had the depth charge been in use, *E-8* would never have made the passage. Without that death knell of the submarine *E-8* was safe against a charging enemy because of the technical adroitness of her crew. The enemy cruiser passed over her forward compartments without touching.

In less than an hour the *E-8* had given the enemy the slip and was again on the surface with the Gulf of Riga on her starboard side. Shortly after midnight on the morning of August 22d, she went to the bottom to wait for daylight. She was now in friendly waters. As the men were finishing breakfast, Dagerort was sighted ahead and, in company with Max Horton's *E-9* and a Russian destroyer, Goodhart's boat passed up the Gulf of Finland. By that night she was safely moored in Revel Harbour.

CHAPTER EIGHT

WITH the arrival of the three E-boats and the coming overland of the C-boats conditions improved for the crews of the British submarines. Latvick became a different place for the British submarine crews located there. The boats had been rarely in port together. The crews were strangers in a country whose tongue was unknown to them and seemed impossible to master. They had lived the life of exiles. With more boats in the Baltic there were always two in port together while the others were out on patrol. The men had an opportunity to enjoy themselves, to see new faces and hear different voices.

It is hard to appreciate how important such matters become to men cooped up inside a submarine for months on end, seeing the same faces day after day, hearing the same voices hour after hour. No matter what the patience of men under such conditions, sooner or later they get on each other's nerves. I remember hearing an officer say one day to one of his crew: "For God's sake don't suck your teeth when you're near me or I'll have you transferred from the boat." The officer had average capacity for suffering in silence; the man was one of the best in the boat. Suddenly an idiosyncrasy had become insupportable. And it was incidents of that kind that made life in submarines so damnable—not bouts with the enemy.

The crews of the E- and C-boats rested while their boats were overhauled and made ready for sea. *E-8* was fitted with a new propeller to replace the one she had lost during her passage into the Baltic. Lieutenant Commander F. N. Cromie in *E-19* and Lieutenant Commander R. C. Halahan in *E-18* arrived at Revel shortly after Goodhart, having successfully accomplished the passage through the sound and through the treacherous waters at the entrance to the Baltic. Their experiences had been no less thrilling than those of their sister ship, *E-8*.

Cromie took command as he was the senior British naval officer in the port. He reorganized the flotilla, and the patrols were worked more systematically. The C-boats were detailed to protect the various Russian ports and anchorages from attack by German ships, and the E-boats were used to patrol those waters where the enemy were most likely to be met and also to harass the trade in iron and magnetic ores carried on between Sweden and Germany. Germany stood in great need of this ore for the manufacture of guns and munitions. The duties of the E-boats were perhaps as arduous as those of boats which operated in the Sea of Marmora. Their chief difficulties came from mine fields laid by the enemy. Every boat patrolling the Baltic had narrow escapes from being blown to smithereens by these fields of hidden death. Lieutenant Commander R. C. Halahan and his crew undoubtedly perished as the result of striking a mine. They went to sea on patrol and were never heard of afterward.

The second danger was their inability to escape attack from enemy destroyers, patrol craft, and other surface ships. The water was so shallow in the Baltic that it was the exception rather than the rule for a submarine on patrol to find herself in sufficient water to submerge deep enough to avoid the searching ram of a ship drawing twenty feet or more.

Every time our submarines made an attack on an enemy ship they accepted the risks of being rammed. After they had fired their torpedoes they could only go to the bottom and pray that the bows of the charging destroyers and cruisers would pass on either side of them. They had also to face bitter

cold, ice and snow in winter and fog in summer.
Add to these difficulties that of operating most of
the time in areas where the enemy had well-protected bases and unlimited craft to patrol the comparatively narrow waters which lie between the
shores of the Baltic and the gulfs of Finland and
Bosnia.

After his arrival at the Russian base no time
was wasted by Lieutenant Commander Goodhart
in getting his boat repaired. A new propeller was
fitted to replace the one he had lost during his
passage into the Baltic. The engines and motors
were also overhauled and everything made ready
for sea again. October 15th found *E-8* heading
toward the waters off Libau. That day she sighted
and stopped the steamer *Margarette* of Königs-
berg, carrying a cargo of iron ore. The crew were
ordered into their boats and the *Margarette* was
sent to the bottom. But this was incidental to the
real purpose of the trip. She arrived off Libau
October 19th and a careful survey of the situation
showed Goodhart that numerous enemy-armed
trawlers and patrol vessels were active behind the
shelter of their mine fields. They were evidently
guarding the entrance to the harbour and the swept
channel which led into it.

Goodhart decided to play the waiting game
and resisted the temptation to engage the smaller
craft. He hoped he might fall in with bigger game

before it was necessary to return from patrol. His patience was rewarded.

During the 22d an armed trawler left the port and after steaming through the swept channel took up a position near one of the outer buoys. At dusk she lit flares. A consultation between the officers on board the British submarine convinced them that she had come out to act the part of lightship or marker.

Hopes ran high and all through the night the crew remained alert, ready to attack the ships they expected to arrive at the port every moment. Dawn came and strengthened into full daylight and the crew thought their hopes were doomed to disappointment. Suddenly smoke appeared on the horizon. It was not from the seaward however but from inside the harbour. The vessels were putting to sea.

When he had decreased his distance sufficiently, Commander Goodhart discovered that the smoke first sighted was from a three-funnelled cruiser with very high masts and from her escorting destroyers, one of which zigzagged ahead on either bow.

Speeding up on the motors, until *E-8* was making more than seven knots, Goodhart steered to intercept the German ships. Timing his attack accurately, he reduced speed so that when he raised the periscope it would not make too much "feather" as it plowed through the calm water. The surface was like a sheet of glass. He was still about three thousand yards away when he saw his quarry in the lense of the periscope. Lowering the instrument, he closed once more to within an estimated distance of fifteen hundred yards. He slowed down again and cautiously raised the periscope. Stooping with his eye to the rubber protecting piece, he raised himself with the instrument and tersely ordered, "Stop raising periscope," the moment it broke surface.

The men at the hydroplanes sat stolidly on their stools before the large wheels which worked the horizontal rudders. Their duty was to keep the boat absolutely steady at twenty feet. The slightest error on their part would offset all their commander's skill. Should she break surface, the boat was surely doomed. Should they allow the boat to sink beyond periscope depth, the instrument might dip below the surface the very moment the enemy came on to the firing course.

As others of the crew rushed to the tubes and flooded them the men at the hydroplanes stayed immovable on their seats, giving the hydroplane wheels the necessary twirl to keep the boat at exactly the right depth.

The periscope was lowered out of sight as the port destroyer passed close ahead of the submarine. Goodhart estimated the enemy's speed at fifteen knots and therefore allowed sufficient time to elapse before he raised the periscope again. He was little more than one thousand yards from the spot the intended victim would pass and if the tip of his periscope was sighted the German ship could probably escape the torpedo by a quick alteration of course.

Finally the moment came and the order was given: "Raise periscope slowly." Every man in the boat stood like an image. Only their commander could see what was going on above them. Less than ten seconds were required for him to complete the final act in the drama. His attack had been perfectly timed. As the periscope broke above the placid sea the forebridge of the enemy ship met with the cross wires of the periscope. One single helm order to allow the necessary deflection and the order "FIRE!" echoed through the boat.

The range was so short that it was impossible for the enemy ship to avoid the torpedo even if she had tried. Only one thing now could rob the Englishmen of success.

Would the torpedo run true? Would it keep its depth?

The first lieutenant, who was the one responsible for the efficiency of the tin fish, held his breath. Would the explosion never materialize?

B-O-O-M!

With a concussion that was plainly felt throughout the boat, the anxiously awaited explosion came.

Through the eyepiece Goodhart saw a dull

flash on the waterline where he expected the torpedo to hit, and then the ship was literally blown skyward. Evidently the torpedo had caused the fore magazine to blow up. So terrific was the explosion that *E-8* had to dive to escape possible damage from the tons of falling débris. She stayed submerged for eight minutes and then rose for another look, but the three-funnelled cruiser had disappeared. Two destroyers were circling around trying to pick up survivors.

Goodhart could have sunk the two destroyers while they were engaged in their errand of mercy as *U-9* had sunk the *Cressy, Hogue,* and *Aboukir* when they stopped to aid each other. Whether it was for humanitarian reasons or because he wanted the enemy to remain in ignorance of the fact that the disaster was due to a submarine and not to a mine will probably never be known. But he left the destroyers alone and headed for his base. The ship he had sunk was the *Prinz Adalbert,* the same vessel Commander Horton had attacked and damaged only a few months before. She was a valuable warship of 9,000 tons register and had just returned to active service after completing her repairs.

(2)

Following this loss, the German naval forces withdrew to an area in the southern Baltic nearer to their lines of communication and larger bases.

Commander Cromie's flotilla now operated to a definite plan—the E-boats to offensive patrols and the ore traffic between Sweden and Germany, and the C-boats, with their shorter cruising range, to patrolling the waters between Libau and Danzig.

Typical of the work done by the E-boats operating against the ore ships was *E-19's* fruitful career on October 11th. She had proceeded on patrol and during the forenoon watch sighted and stopped the *Walter Leonhardt*. To do this she had naturally to come to the surface in what were actually enemy waters. She had to take the chance of being torpedoed by an enemy submarine and the chance that the innocent-looking merchantman was in reality an armed vessel flying false colours. I mention these possibilities to point out how the crews of submarines belonging to both countries were always on the *qui vive*. They were always under tension; always suffering nervous strain. The *Walter Leonhardt* proved to be bound from Lulea to Hamburg with iron ore. She was legitimate prey. Cromie ordered her crew into the boats. Our men felt about sinking merchant ships as a big game hunter would feel if he were to turn his rifle on a domestic cow in a barnyard. Attacking warships was a different matter. They were swift of speed and deadly in defense. Hunting them brought a thrill no big-game hunter ever experienced.

From the conning tower Cromie saw that the weather was growing threatening. Ordering the crew of the ore ship to remain where they were in their lifeboats, he chased off to investigate smoke on the horizon. He found a Swedish vessel, stopped her, and requested that she alter course to pick up the crew of the *Water Leonhardt.*

Hardly had the huge ore ship settled to the bottom than another ship was sighted. She turned tail the moment she sighted *E-19* and raced for the beach. Cromie went alongside the stranded vessel and, making fast to her, tried to tow her into sufficient water to sink her. Failing in this, he ordered the crew ashore and damaged the ship to such an extent that salvage would be out of the question. The *Germania* had 3,000 tons of ore aboard of her.

Just as the men were trying to snatch a bite to eat *E-19* stopped the *Gutrune.* Her papers showed her to be bound from Lulea to Hamburg. She was sent to the bottom with 4,400 tons of ore. Before sinking her, Cromie placed her crew aboard a Swedish steamer. Within the hour he was hot on the trail of two more large steamers. The first he reached was a Swedish vessel, and as her papers were all correct she was allowed to proceed. *E-19* chased after the other which turned out to be the *Direktor Rippenhagen* loaded with magnetic ore for Germany. While she was in the process of sinking he stopped another ship which was bound for Newcastle, England, and put the crew of the *Direktor* aboard. Hardly was this job finished when the *Nicodemia* hove into view. As soon as she sighted the submarine she altered course and headed for the coast of Sweden, hoping to gain the protection of neutral waters. A couple of shots aimed close to her bows made her change her mind and her crew was forced to watch the cargo of nearly seven thousand tons go crashing downward as the extremely well-appointed ship surrendered to the charges which had been put aboard her. As no other ship was near, *E-19* towed the crew to shore. Cromie had destroyed more than twenty-two thousand tons of enemy shipping that day and had made ample provision for the safety of the crews of the destroyed vessels.

Days such as this were not uncommon, and before long caused a panic among enemy and neutral shipping. Captains of destroyers and armed trawlers were informed that the sinking of a British submarine would be considered equal in importance to the sinking of a Russian battleship. In the anxiety to make a kill some crews overreached, as happened when a Danish submarine was mistaken for a British boat and fire was opened on her, killing the navigating officer who was on the conning tower.

During the forenoon of November 7, 1915, Lieutenant Commander Cromie sighted two destroyers and a cruiser escorting the large ferryboat *Preussin*. He speeded up to head them off but failed to intercept them and they passed out of range of his torpedoes. From the way they avoided him, it was thought that they must have seen either his conning tower or his periscope. At a little after 1 P. M. while a mist made for poor visibility, he ran into what he took to be a cruiser and one destroyer. Perhaps the fog hid the other destroyer from view but the two were of the same convoy he had seen during the morning. Whatever the facts, he took no chance of missing them the second time. This attack took him to within one thousand yards of his enemy and the torpedo he fired struck her starboard side well forward. As the torpedo hit, Cromie saw her pivot around almost in a circle. Then she seemed to stop dead. She was on fire and evidently sinking, but Cromie had a great respect for the manner in which Germany constructed her ships. He avoided the rush of the escorting destroyer and at great risk dived right under the stern of the sinking vessel, feeling reasonably sure that the destroyer would still be hunting him on the other side. He brought *E-19* up to periscope depth and, aiming below the cruiser's mainmast, delivered her death blow.

The torpedo struck just above where it was aimed, and when the German vessel blew up, débris was thrown to a height of two hundred feet into the air.

While Cromie was trying to make out the identity of his kill the destroyer sighted *E-19's* periscope and opened fire on it with high-explosive shells. The periscope was lowered, just to put them

off their aim, and three minutes later Cromie took
another look to see what was happening, but the
cruiser had gone . . . to the bottom. The destroyer
steamed about picking up a number of survivors.
She seemed very restless and rarely stayed more
than a few seconds in any one position. The German ferryboat came along and the destroyer de-
parted hurriedly for the southward, leaving the
ferryboat to complete the work of rescue.

Cromie's victim turned out to be the cruiser
Undine of 2,650 tons. Reporting the matter officially, Cromie gave all the credit to his subordinate,
Lieutenant G. Sharpe, who was officer of the watch
at the time the enemy was sighted. Cromie stated
that the whole success was due to the alertness of
this officer in seeing the enemy before being seen
and on his sound judgment in estimating the course
and speed correctly in the very short time he had
at his disposal. Had he failed in any of these
things, the chances, owing to the fog and low
visibility, were that the enemy would have escaped
for the second time that day.

All submarine commanders who served under
Cromie did equally well during their time in the
Baltic. Not all had the satisfaction of bagging an
enemy warship, but that was hardly their fault.
Enemy warships did not put to sea more than was
absolutely necessary. All our boats did good work,
however, against the iron-ore traffic, and by en-
forcing the blockade, kept the enemy from being

as aggressive as he might have been had there been no British submarines in the Baltic.

The latter phases of the Baltic operations are concerned so much with Commander Cromie that it is worth the space to tell something of his character. His men always said that they would have "followed the 'owner' to hell and back." He was an ideal submarine officer, more accomplished than most in the technical side of his work, quiet in speech, courageous as a lion, and always willing to take a sporting chance; the type of officer, in short, that is idolized by British seamen.

One day when on patrol off Memel, Cromie, and his whole crew probably, grew very bored with the monotony of the job. No ships were moving. Nothing had happened to break the dull routine of eating, sleeping, and watching. Behind the defenses that guarded the harbour entrance many enemy vessels were probably anchored. To attempt an entrance was foolhardy, perhaps, but it was enticing too. Cromie put the proposition up to his crew fairly and squarely. "The risk is great," he said. "Do you want to take that risk? If we are lucky we may achieve a great success. If we fail we shall probably lose the boat and our lives."

The seaman who told me the story said: "We told him, 'Right-oh! Lead on, McDuff,' we says, and gor blimey, he did. We got stuck so fast in the blinkin' nets they had placed across the channel mouth that if they hadn't all been asleep on those there German boats our goose would have been cooked good and plenty."

For hours Cromie and his crew did everything possible to extricate themselves from the mess they had gotten into. No matter what they did, no matter how they tried, the submarine remained hopelessly entangled. When the batteries were finally running low and the chances of breaking free were negligible, Cromie sent for all members of his crew and spoke to them in the control room of the boat. "Men," he said, "it looks as if our chances of breaking adrift are very small. I'm going to put everything we have into one last effort. If we do not get free then I intend to rise to the surface and give you a chance for your lives. The blame for what has happened is entirely mine. I'm sorry."

Cromie was then prepared to sacrifice his life in the interests of his country, as he did afterward. He placed charges around the hull of the boat and near the warheads of the torpedoes. Should his last effort to clear the boat from her entanglements fail he would take her to the surface and give the crew a chance of being rescued by some of the boats who were busy trying to blow them up. He intended to remain behind and personally carry out the destruction of his boat. But this sacrifice was not necessary. With the last ounce of juice, with the last frantic rush of the propellers, the wires parted and they drifted free, to escape death once more.

But the dark clouds of revolution were gathering over the eastern front. Insidious Red propaganda was undermining the morale of the Russian Navy. It is to the credit of the British crews that they conducted themselves in a manner of which Britain could be proud. They were then allies of the Russian nation. Russia's political affairs were none of their business. Much as they might have liked to interfere, they obeyed the orders of their officers and kept themselves apart. And all through the winter of 1915-16 those men uncomplainingly put to sea and carried on, performing their dangerous duties while the spirit was gradually sapped from the crews of the Russian ships.

The men's devotion to duty was inspiring. An ice breaker had to precede them in and out of harbour. At sea in the bitter cold, they had to perform patrols rightfully the duty of the crews of the Russian submarines which rarely if ever left harbour. When conditions became too bad in the German submarine service toward the middle of 1918 the U-boat crews mutinied as did the Russians in 1916, but did either of them perform tasks as difficult as our men did in the Baltic and Dardanelles?

Lieutenant Command Halahan and his crew in *E-18* paid the extreme price. They went to sea in May, 1916, and never returned. After escaping death in a dozen different forms all winter, they evidently fell victims to moored mines in the spring of the year.

As the hideous spectacle of revolution developed, Cromie found himself in the position where he had to witness his own Russian servant being chosen to command the ship he was aboard. He had to witness his friends among the Russian naval officers being insulted and brutally treated. But the Russians themselves had such a regard for the conduct and bravery of the British officers and men that orders were issued that none of them was to be molested. The order was issued with dire threats in the event of disobedience.

One seaman of the revolutionary navy did break the order. He insulted a British officer who reported the matter to the Sailors' Council. The man was arrested and would have been executed had the officer he insulted not pleaded for his life. After the death sentence had been quashed the luckless individual was brought across to the E-boat on which the officer served and his guards made him go on his knees and apologize before the boat's crew. Then they forced his face to the steel decks and rubbed his nose vigorously up and down and crossways at the commander's feet. This over, he was exiled to Siberia for an indefinite period. The very men involved in this ludicrous act of discipline had but recently murdered numbers of their own officers after subjecting them to the most horrible insults and degradation. They had even poured a can of lamp oil over their admiral and

set him afire while they danced around him like a
bunch of dervishes.

It seems impossible to believe half the stories
our men brought back from the Baltic when, after
destroying all the British and Russian submarines
to prevent their falling into the hands of the Germans, they returned to continue their duties in new
boats which were being constructed in the ship-
yards at home.

One story is told of the council ordering one of
the Russian submarines to sea. While leaving harbour the man in command ordered a practice dive.
This was a sane and sensible thing to do according
to the practice of the British Navy. But the order
happened to come at "stand-easy time." The man
whose duty it was to close the after hatch was en-
joying his stand-easy. Under the new conditions,
how could anybody dare give an order during such
a time? The idea was preposterous, so he ignored
the order and the boat dived with the hatch open.
The boat stayed down. The Red sailor was a man
ready to die for his principles, whatever the cost.
By some freak the man in command of the boat and
the second in command were saved and both after
court-martial were sent to Siberia. The attitude of
those appointed to inquire into the loss of the submarine was that the order to "dive" was harsh and
unreasonable, considering that the men were having their "stand-easy time" and could not therefore
be reasonably expected to carry out the order.

While this nightmare continued, Cromie carried on. He did his utmost to keep the fighting forces on the side of the Allies. Such was his influence with the revolutionary sailors that they committed no excesses or murders in the port of Revel where Cromie was stationed. This was in direct contrast to the bloody debacle which went on in Helsingfors and other Russian naval bases.

Not only did he keep the British submarines operating against the enemy in the hope that some miracle might happen to give the Russians control of themselves once again, as men recover from a drunken stupor, but he mastered the Russian language as well and conducted many interesting and important diplomatic undertakings of great value to the Allies. And when the day arrived when the Russians signed the separate treaty with Germany demanding, as part of the agreement, the surrender of our submarines, Cromie saw to it that they were taken to sea and went to the bottom and to safety. They sank to the noise of their own thunder.

On the morning of April 8th, rather than surrender the flotilla to the enemy as required by the terms of the separate peace treaty, Cromie ordered all the British boats to sea. They were escorted by a surface vessel manned by a crew friendly to the British officers and men. Demolition charges were placed throughout the hulls of the submarines. Fuses were attached to the war heads of the torpedoes lying in their tubes. When everything was ready the crews stepped from the decks of the boats they had learned to love to the deck of the rescue vessel. The time fuses were lit. They sizzled down below, creeping nearer and nearer to the explosives in the boats. The Russian boat with the British crews on board steamed farther away, then stopped and all eyes gazed back at the little fleet of seven submarines patiently awaiting their doom. It was like killing a dog which had served one faithfully and had grown too old to be of further use. Suddenly, there was a terrific flash. Sheets of flame like arms reached beseechingly to the skies. Then a pall of dark heavy smoke settled down over the sea. The muffled roar of the explosion rumbled over the water to the ears of the watching crews who had served the cause so faithfully under such trying circumstances. It was the end. As the gentle breeze wafted away the smoky shroud which hung over the tragic scene, the steel gray waters looked placid and calm except for occasional bubbles that rose from the ocean's floor.

With the submarines at the bottom of the Baltic, most of the officers and crews returned home to England. Because of his knowledge of the Russian language and his great influence with the Russian revolutionaries, Cromie remained on, doing his best to stay the madness which was so endangering the Allied cause. And his efforts were not in vain. He saved hundreds, perhaps thousands, of lives, and when he died it was on the steps of the British Embassy at Petrograd as a man might wish to die. Single-handed he disputed the entrance of an infuriated mob until they tramped across his bleeding body to burn and plunder.

CHAPTER NINE

ALTHOUGH the operations of the Trade in the
Baltic and in the Sea of Marmora contain as splendid exploits of boats and men as are known to naval
history, both campaigns take their places in the
naval phase of the Great War as superb sideshows.
They demonstrate the courage and skill of the British Navy and Naval Reserve in operating the craft
which was Germany's only effective naval arm during the war. They illustrate certain uses of the submarine which never came to light through the
German usage of the weapon. At the time, they
were the cause of considerable embarrassment to
the enemy, and, in so far as the boats accomplished
their objectives, were successful, but the reader
must remember that both operations took place

before the depth charge was invented, and that had
this terrible and effective weapon against the submarine been in the hands of Turkey and Germany
in 1914 and 1915, the record of the Trade's success in the Baltic and the Sea of Marmora would
read very differently. It is doubtful if one boat in
ten could have forced the Dardanelles or one in
four the Baltic.

In any case, the Trade's main show was in the
home waters of the North Sea where submersibles
played their devious secretive rôles as eyes of the
Grand Fleet and the first line of defense against
the diffident German Navy. In the mine-infested
waters off the British Isles our submarines had a
titanic task to perform. From the moment of the
declaration of the war until the German U-boats,
like prisoners in a chain gang, steamed into Harwich, they were constantly on patrol, keeping the
seas in all weathers, praying at all times for sight
of German battle craft, and, as outposts secreted
on the sea thresholds of the enemy, rendering in-
valuable aid to the high command of the British
Grand Fleet. In the home waters their duties were
threefold. First, they patrolled the areas in and
around the Bight of Heligoland and the entrance
to the Baltic. While performing these duties they
kept a strict lookout for enemy ships, and when
any were sighted outward bound in squadrons they
came to the surface and reported the strength, position, course, and speed of the enemy fleet to the

commander in chief by wireless. The pious hope was to bring about a general fleet action. Our submarines were not allowed to attack an enemy fleet outward bound. It was considered far more desirable to pass on the information to forces which might be able to make a clean-up of a whole squadron should contact be established.

Our boats also maintained a vigilant watch on the smaller craft employed by the enemy in minesweeping duties, and compiled valuable information as to the disposition of his protective mine fields, and swept channels. Other boats acted as mine layers. They took their deadly cargoes well into the Bight and laid them where they were likely to do most harm. All boats on patrol attacked enemy submarines whenever an opportunity was offered. The officers and crews of the Trade sank more enemy U-boats than any other single branch of the service. Eighteen in all fell victims to their well-aimed torpedoes.

When luck was with us, and one of our boats on patrol met single ships of the enemy or squadrons returning to their base, we attacked. Some wonderful and spectacular feats were performed against the capital ships of the enemy fleet, but it was unfortunate that on most occasions the damage done by the torpedo was not sufficient to sink the larger vessels. Many were able to make port in a seriously damaged condition.

The patrols of overseas boats were organized so

that each submarine did about fourteen days at
sea and the same number in port. When they returned from patrol half the crew got three days'
leave and the other half, with the help of the per-
manent depot staff, worked at reconditioning the
boat. When those on leave returned, the boat went
on standby duty, ready to help the smaller and
older boats engaged in coastal-defense duties.

The story of the North Sea operations is as much
a story of men sealed in unsavoury tin cans, wal-
lowing around a shallow ocean and continually at
war with Nature, as it is a story of dramatic en-
counters between craft of opposing navies. In this
respect, the experience of the German submarine
officers and men must have been identical with our
own.

Before conquering the enemy each had to conquer Nature. The difficulties of submarine navigation in sea areas notorious for their tides and currents, the fury of their storms, the voidless blanket-
ing of their fogs were tremendous. Most patrols
were made submerged in shallow waters which,
when gales raged, were stirred to motion to the
very sea bed. When this happened the action
known in submarines as pumping followed. Pumping is to a submarine what air pockets are to an
airplane. Under water the danger of loosening
plates and destroying the buoyancy of the boat is
similar to that of falling in an airplane out of control. Heavy weather in the North Sea demanded

every ounce of skill and patience officers and men could call upon to keep their boats under control on or near the surface. It was more difficult to sit on the bottom in an effort to escape the wave motion.

Often for days on end the navigators were prevented from getting sun sights either by dark and cloudy weather or by the activities of enemy patrol vessels. Most of the peace-time aids to navigation, such as lightships, buoys, and land marks, had been removed and most lighthouses no longer flashed warning signals to ships at sea. Added to natural dangers, the overseas boats met those of enemy mine fields, speedy patrol craft, and lurking enemy submarines. From the middle of 1915 onward the North Sea, particularly the southern section of it, was one gigantic mine field. These floating globes of death undoubtedly accounted for the twenty-odd British submarines which went on patrol never to return and never to be heard of again.

In winter the boats were like defective ice houses and in summer almost unbearable from gassing batteries and foul air. When the boats pitched and rolled on the surface while charging their batteries every man in them fell a victim to serious spells of nausea. Most men had very slight appetite for food and were unable to retain what little they took. There is no question in a submarine of men being good sailors, or finding their sea legs. Few human beings have the cast-iron insides that could survive, in addition to the worn-out air, the pitching, reeling, tossing antics of a submarine in foul weather. The submarine would roll through an arc of fifty to sixty degrees in a matter of a few seconds with a quick corkscrew motion that upset the strongest stomachs.

Notwithstanding these distresses, we found when men needed discipline, which they rarely did, that it was only necessary to tell them that if they didn't watch themselves they would be returned to the general service. Thus threatened, a miraculous change was wrought, for in the Trade no greater humiliation could be suffered than to be kicked out of it by transfer. Both officers and men were volunteers. Not only volunteers, but the pick of all those who did volunteer. The standard required by those who did the choosing was so high that only a little better than 50 per cent. were accepted. Yet never during the whole of the war was there ever a shortage of the finest type of men to fill the vacancies caused by the increased construction programme, by illness, accidents, and deaths in action.

(2)

While the world was just recovering from the shock of the declaration of war, Britain's submarines were returning from their first trip into the Bight. Those were strenuous days. Hardly were boats overhauled before they were on their way to sea again. The information gained by those initial patrols were the basis of the tactics which developed into the Battle of the Bight in which submarines *E-4, -5, -6, -7, -8, -9* were detailed to play a most important part.

During the first patrols the submarines had discovered that every evening enemy light cruisers escorted to sea a number of destroyers. The destroyers spread out fanlike for their nightly patrols, evidently seeking to destroy our submarines while charging their batteries. It had also been ascertained that these ships rendezvoused each morning in a position about twenty miles northwest of Heligoland before returning to their base. The information was obtained at considerable risk, and it was only sheer bad luck that prevented one of our boats sinking a large cruiser of the *Roon* type on the morning of August 21st. On the other hand, several of our submarines had hairbreadth escapes from ramming by enemy vessels. So honours were easy.

Commodore Keyes, who commanded the 8th or overseas submarine flotilla, after receiving the information brought back by his patrols, submitted to his senior officers a plan to involve the enemy patrol ships in an action.

The intention was to bring about an engagement between the enemy patrol boats and our own forces. Three submarines were to lie in ambush for the enemy, and three others were to offer them-

selves as bait to entice the enemy ships into the trap
prepared for them.

It was the practice in those early days of the war
for the submarine commodore to accompany his
boats to sea and direct their operations from. the
bridge of a destroyer, the *Lurcher*. It was as the result of experience gained in this and other actions
that the K-class submarines were constructed. It
was learned that E-class submarines had not the
necessary speed, either when on the surface or submerged, to coöperate successfully with surface
ships. The K-boats were constructed so that they
could perform the dual rôle of destroyer and submarine. They were capable of developing twenty-
five knots on the surface and ten to twelve submerged. They could thus keep up with the battle
fleet which had a speed of about twenty-one knots.
They also were as heavily armed as most destroyers. Unfortunately they never had an opportunity
to demonstrate what their capabilities against an
enemy fleet actually were.

The Battle of the Bight was originally staged
for the benefit of our submarines, but the surface
ships were not able to chase or lead the enemy into
the positions in which our boats waited patiently
for an opportunity to attack.

Three E-boats, *4, 5*, and *9*, were detailed to take
up positions near Heligoland, from which they
could attack any enemy vessels entering or leaving.
E-6, E-7, and *E-8* were allotted the pleasant task of

acting as decoys. Their instructions were to take up a position some forty miles out from the German base. There they were to expose themselves in an effort to entice enemy destroyer patrols to attack.

The action off Heligoland, as the Battle of the Bight is usually known, became somewhat confused because signals intended for senior officers never reached them. As a result, one half the ships engaged never knew what the other half was doing or what they themselves were supposed to be doing.

In the thick of the action Lieutenant Commander Leir, R. N., in command of *E-4,* had one of the most extraordinary experiences that ever fell to the lot of a submarine captain. I served under Commander Leir in 1918. I was navigating officer of Submarine *K-12,* and he was in charge of the Firth of Forth submarine flotilla of K-boats operating with the battle-cruiser squadrons.

The plans matured and the enemy patrols attacked. Commodore W. E. Goodenough, commanding six light cruisers, joined in the scrap, which had developed into a series of dog fights staged on a mist-enshrouded sea. He did not know that our submarines were taking part in the operations. On the alert for enemy submarines, and not knowing our own boats were in the vicinity, Commodore Goodenough sighted *E-6* and promptly tried to ram her. Only the peace-time practice of training submarine crews to operate with the fleet

during manœuvres saved *E-6*. Thanks to it, Lieutenant Commander Talbot was able to dive in sufficient time to allow the flagship to pass over him
without doing any real damage. Notwithstanding
the excitement, the cool-headed commander of *E-6*
recognized the vessel looming up out of the fog
and did not make the same mistake as the flagship
had. He might easily have retaliated and sunk her
with a torpedo.

While this little drama was enacted the German
destroyer *V-187* fell victim to the gunnery of our
surface ships. Lieutenant Commander Leir, patrolling submerged, saw all this happen through
his periscope. Cut off from the rest of her flotilla,
the unfortunate destroyer put up a splendid fight
against overwhelming numbers. Seeing that she
was hopelessly crippled and liable to sink at any
moment, our light cruisers lowered two boats and
sent them to help with the work of rescue. But if
the enemy had fought gallantly, he certainly
showed a lack of chivalry. The destroyer opened
fire on the boats going to the rescue of her crew.
An officer on the enemy destroyer was seen to train
and fire one of the undamaged guns at H. M. S.
Goshawk, also preparing to aid in the work of rescue. The shell crashed into *Goshawk's* wardroom
when she was less than two hundred yards away.

The British immediately opened fire again, intending to put the offending gun out of action,
but the vessel sank. The boats again closed to pick

up the survivors. They were engaged in this work
of mercy when an enemy cruiser showed up out of
the mist and opened a heavy fire. It was impossible
to continue the work of rescue, but despite all that
had happened it was decided to take our men back
on board but leave our boats behind, so that those
of the enemy who had been picked up might save
some of their comrades still swimming in the water.

By this time the action was raging hotly and it
was necessary for our ships to move off to keep in
touch with the enemy. One cutter with its crew had
to be left behind, miles from land, in enemy waters, with little hope of rescue. What might have
happened to them is hard to surmise if it hadn't
been for *E-4*. Having witnessed all this through the
periscope, Leir made an attack on the enemy
cruiser *Stettin* when she arrived, but the torpedo
missed as the cruiser made a quick alteration in
course. She then steered straight for the attacking
submarine and forced her to dive. When Leir came
to the surface again he found that the sailors left
behind by the *Defender* had stripped themselves to
the waist and were using their clothing for band-
ages; they were busily engaged binding up the
wounds of the German seamen they had rescued.
The E-boat took on board the members of the
Defender's crew, together with one German officer
and two prisoners—as a sample, Leir explained
afterward. Water and biscuits were left for the seamen he was forced to leave behind.

Owing to the weather conditions and other factors which developed, none of the other submarines became engaged. The action was still raging
up and down the Bight. Heavy fog banks hung low
in patches over the water when Admiral Beatty
with his battle cruisers raced into the mêlée. He
steered for the sound of gunfire, certain that the
enemy would send out his battle cruisers to drive
off our lighter craft. The *Arethusa* and her attached destroyers had just left the sinking German
Mainz for Commodore Goodenough to finish off
when they sighted two large enemy ships, the *Köln*
and the *Stettin*. These two vessels alone were more
than a match for our lightly armed craft and when
they saw the huge shapes of battle cruisers loom
out of the fog the destroyers thought their game
was up.

The *Arethusa,* banging away at two ships twice
her size, was doing one of those little stunts which
earned her the title: *Saucy Arethusa*. What a re-
lief it was to recognize the new arrivals as Admiral Beatty's ships. The German ships turned and
ran, but their running did them no good. The German flagship *Köln* was reduced to a flaming ruin.
The *Stettin* disappeared into the fog and smoke to
the northward. Just as the *Köln* burst into flame
another shape loomed up out of the fog—the little
Ariadne.

Leaving the *Köln,* Beatty's ships took after the
new arrival. She wriggled and zigzagged to shake

off her impending doom, but the first salvo of
heavy shells wiped her out of existence. Having
completed the task of extracting the rest of the
British forces from the tight corner in which they
had placed themselves owing to the failure of the
signals to reach their destination, Admiral Beatty
gave the signal: "Retire."

Retracing their course, they once again came
across the crippled *Köln*. She was still flying her
colours defiantly at her masthead. There was nothing to do but finish her. The second salvo crashed
home. Beatty ordered four destroyers to the spot
to rescue the crew but it was futile. All they found
was one lone stoker. The flotilla admiral and his
complement of 380 men had perished.

Meanwhile the *Mainz* fought her guns until,
owing to her heavy list, they were pointing skyward. Commodore Keyes, commanding the submarines engaged in the action, closed in on the
sinking ship with his two destroyers, the *Lurcher*
and the *Firedrake*.

They had started to rescue the men who were
jumping overboard when our men were horrified
to see the officers of the *Mainz* shooting in the
back those of their men who attempted to jump.
Commodore Keyes couldn't stand it. At great
risk he ordered the *Lurcher* to be laid alongside. His crew swarmed onto the decks of the burning German ship and, regardless of the risk they

themselves ran, succeeded in removing all the survivors except two officers who absolutely refused to leave their ship. Hardly had the task of mercy been completed than the *Mainz* turned over on her beam ends and went down so suddenly that she nearly took the *Lurcher* with her. The two officers who had remained on board were picked up by a boat from the light cruiser *Liverpool*. Three hundred and forty-eight officers and men were rescued from the *Mainz* out of her total complement of 380. Sixty of the survivors were wounded, many of them mortally. Several bore wounds in the back where they had been shot by their own officers.

The total losses suffered by the enemy in this action was the *Frauenlob*, 50 men; the *V-187*, 50; the *Mainz*, 32; the *Köln*, 380; and the *Ariadne* 275—in addition to killed and wounded aboard other vessels which got back to port. Our losses were negligible. Notwithstanding the fact that she was twice engaged in single combat with two of the enemy, the *Saucy Arethusa* lost only one officer and ten men killed and one officer and sixteen wounded. In the destroyers and other ships engaged, the losses were so slight that the total, including the *Arethusa's*, came to thirty-five killed and forty wounded.

It is hard to say what our submarines would have done had the plans matured as originally intended. As it was, they did not have half a chance.

The visibility was so poor that those boats which did sight surface ships lost them again in the fog or mist before they could properly identify them.

It is no easy matter to distinguish friend from foe among the smaller type and class of warships, even when conditions are favourable. During the hours the action was fought, with the exception of *E-4* and *E-6,* those at the periscopes in the British submarines saw nothing at all or only just caught a glimpse of grayish shadows speeding through blankets of mist and fog.

Admiral Jellicoe recognized that submarines could be better employed patrolling certain defined positions regularly than dodging about with surface ships. As the war progressed these patrols were organized, and when an action between the two fleets was pending all submarines went to certain pre-arranged "fleet-action positions" and stayed there. These positions commanded strategical positions likely to be used by the enemy surface ships, but our own ships kept clear of them, thus avoiding confusion.

Shortly after this action *E-7* was ordered to the Dardanelles, and *E-8* and *E-9* later distinguished themselves in the Baltic. The other three boats that took part in the first real naval battle of the war continued their patrols in the North Sea, and two of them, *E-5* and *E-6,* were later destroyed in the mine fields through which they were constantly forced to navigate.

(3)

Dull monotonous patrols enlivened by stunts like the Bight affair were the lot of E-boats operating out of Harwich. A stunt was a dramatic interlude of action continually longed for and eagerly embraced. Such a stunt occurred when German battle cruisers attacked the Yorkshire coast on December 16, 1914, and shelled Hartlepool and Scarborough. Submarine *C-9* was in Hartlepool Harbour. The raid was so sudden and unexpected that she was taken completely unawares when shells began to fall at 8:15 A.M.

C-9's commander, Lieutenant C. L. Y. Deering, immediately headed for sea to attack the enemy ships. Unfortunately, it was low tide and there was less than eighteen feet of water over the bar. This meant he had to run out on the surface and as he proceeded as requisite the enemy put up a heavy barrage of shell fire across the harbour entrance. Nothing daunted, the old C-boat steered right for the gap, and as tons of metal churned the water all around her she scraped over the bar, dived and bumped down the sand bank into deeper water. The crew went to action stations as the C-boat gained sufficient water to enable her to trim for diving. There weren't any happier men in the British Navy than her crew. For once they had all had a chance to see what they were after. They had seen the three large enemy battle cruisers loom up out of the mist; they had heard the shells passing through the air; they had seen them burst in the town behind; they had heard the terrified screams of women and children as they rushed out of their humble homes in the poorer districts down by the waterfront; and as they slipped their moorings and headed for sea they saw house after house collapse like a pack of cards, burying helpless victims who rushed distracted to the streets.

Moving at full speed, *C-9* faced the shell fire and miraculously escaped damage and headed straight for the *Blücher*. Her crew were doomed to disappointment, however, for the enemy ships, seeing that she had made her way out of the harbour, turned and made off to the eastward. Our men had the satisfaction of knowing, however, that they had been instrumental in saving many lives; for the casualties inflicted on the inhabitants of Hartlepool, in the short time the German ships were left unmolested, amounted to 86 killed and 424 wounded.

Following the raid, Commodore Keyes set out in the H.M.S. *Lurcher,* taking seven British submarines and the French submarine *Archimede* with him to await the enemy's return home. The British submarines in this stunt were *E-2, -7, -8, -10, -11,* and *-15.* They proceeded to Heligoland and off the entrance to the German rivers the Jade, the Ems, and the Weser.

Lieutenant Commander Nasmith in *E-11* was in

the southernmost position. He was in line off the
Weser, and as he patrolled at periscope depth,
anxiously waiting for something to turn up, he
found himself within sight of numerous enemy destroyers chasing about at full speed, apparently
searching the approaches to the harbour for possible submarines. He kept a careful watch and tried
to keep his periscope from being seen. This was
not easy, for a nasty short sea was running and
heavy pumping made it extremely difficult to keep
the boat under control.

At last the leading ships of Admiral Hipper's
squadron were sighted through the periscope and
Nasmith started his attack. Evading the swarm of
escorting destroyers by diving right under them,
he came to periscope depth within four hundred
yards of the leading enemy ship and let go his torpedo, but the short steep seas caused the torpedo
to run badly and it passed under its target before
it had recovered its proper running depth.

The imperturbable Nasmith then concentrated
his efforts against the third ship of the line and got
to within five hundred yards of her, but the alarm
had been given and *E-11* had to go crashing to the
bottom to avoid the ram of the ship as she altered
course and steamed at full speed right over the top
of the E-boat.

To escape the immediate danger, he had been
forced to flood all tanks, which naturally put the

boat completely out of diving trim. Disappointed at the failure of his attack, he worked feverishly to trim the boat again and get her to periscope depth, hoping to get in another attack before the capital ships would evade him altogether.

When he again got into position to see what was going on above, he found the enemy boats in a panic, with destroyers dashing about in all directions to cover the retreat of the larger ships. Weaving his way through them, missing their sharp bows by mere inches, he succeeded in getting within range again and made an attack on the rear ship of the enemy line. His persistence and nerve were not to be rewarded however. Once more the speeding torpedo was avoided.

All this happened on the morning of December 16th. After waiting all next day without any enemy ships showing themselves, the British submarines and their French consort were ordered to return to harbour. They arrived back December 19th.

Within a week they were out to sea again, this time coöperating with the surface ships and air force in a raid on Cuxhaven. Only those who have served in submarines can have any idea of the strain the crews suffered when putting in so much sea time during the early days of the war. The principal object of this raid was to try and bring about a fleet action and to give our submarines a chance to demonstrate their effectiveness as engines of war.

In this raid it fell to the lot of *E-11's* crew to have all the excitement again. She was patrolling submerged off Norderney when Commander Nasmith saw a seaplane drop into the sea. Coming to the surface, he made toward her and found her a British plane forced down by lack of fuel and oil. He took the pilot aboard his boat and the plane in tow, although enemy patrol boats, submarines, and aircraft were known to be in the vicinity.

While they were proceeding on the surface with the plane in tow the pilot told his story. He was one of the nine pilots who had been escorted off the enemy coast by a suitable force of surface ships. Their objective had been the zeppelin sheds at Cuxhaven. They had arrived in position on Christmas morning. The weather conditions appeared perfect. There was little wind and the sun was shining as they took off from the decks of their parent ships. Unfortunately, two of the machines failed to take off and only seven were able to take part in the raid.

The perfect weather conditions experienced while over the sea did not hold good over the land. Hardly had they crossed the coast line when they encountered a heavy fog. The pilot told how the flight had become separated and how he had flown about seeking his objective.

He explained how, failing to locate the zeppelin sheds, he had dropped his bombs on one of the enemy bases and then flown over the Schilling Roads where he had sighted a main part of the enemy fleet, consisting of seven battleships and three battle cruisers, at anchor.

For reasons best known to himself, the enemy did not attempt to interfere with the raid or with the supporting ships except to send out zeppelins and a squadron of airplanes. Otherwise, he would have found himself trapped between the Grand Fleet and the submarines which were placed to ambush the enemy vessels when they attempted to return to port.

Before the pilot of the seaplane finished his story two more British machines landed on the water near *E-11*. They too were out of fuel. As they taxied over toward the boat a zeppelin was seen heading toward them at full speed. Nasmith was in a nasty position, and had to make up his mind quickly what to do. With his typical disregard for danger he ignored the zeppelin and proceeded to strip the most valuable parts from the machine he was towing and then headed toward the others to rescue their pilots.

The zeppelin was somewhat inquisitive, however, and swooped low over the submarine. To gain more time Nasmith paused in his work, took his cap off, and waved a cheery greeting to the crew overhead. The zeppelin commander was on the point of dropping his bombs when Nasmith waved. Doubt entered the German's mind. Surely no one but a U-boat captain would risk such a friendly gesture. Before he could make up his mind as to the nationality of the boat below him, the airship had passed and had to turn again, when the mistake was established, before dropping its bombs. The time taken in turning allowed Nasmith to complete the work of taking the British pilots aboard.

As he completed his task and *E-11* dipped under the water, the zeppelin overhead dropped two bombs. The explosions were distinctly felt by those in the submarine but no damage resulted. While the zeppelin was engrossed with *E-11, D-6,* another of our submarines under the command of Lieutenant Commander R. C. Halahan, came to the surface and didn't dive again until she was satisfied that the disabled seaplanes had been sunk. *D-6* was herself sunk by an enemy submarine on the 26th of June, 1918, after surviving four years of constant warfare, and she was credited with having sunk *UB-72* in 1918 just before she met her own fate.

These stunts give an idea of the home life of our undersea boats during the early days of the war. An idea of the terrible weather conditions they experienced is given by the fact that the Admiralty decided to discontinue sending them into the shallow waters of the Bight during stormy weather. The terrible pumping made boats almost unmanageable, and to patrol at periscope depth, without continually breaking surface, impossible. It was found also that no torpedo would run straight in the short, choppy seas generally experienced off the coasts of Germany during the winter months.

CHAPTER TEN

WHILE the overseas flotillas were operating with
the fleet and keeping diving patrols off the Bight
of Heligoland, our older and smaller submarines
were having plenty of work to do nearer to home.
The C-boats were good diving boats but they had
only a small cruising radius. They did wonderful
work considering their handicaps and provided
the best possible medium for training young officers who were later appointed to command larger
overseas boats.

Until the end of 1914, the C-boats were used
principally to patrol the Strait of Dover and
watch for enemy submarines and destroyers which
might have designs on the transports carrying
troops over to France. They also did what were
known as coastal defense patrols.

In doing this they performed a valuable service.
The enemy was actively mining the entrance to
Harwich, the Thames, the waters off the Belgian
coast, and the approaches to the Strait of Dover.
Often our submarines were the first to locate these
mine fields. When boats failed to return from patrol mine sweepers would be sent to sweep in
the areas and they seldom returned without locat-
ing a nest of eggs, overripe and ready to cause
trouble.

After the H.M.S. *Formidable* had been sunk by
an enemy submarine while exercising in the Channel on New Year's night, 1915, with the loss of 547
officers and men, the Admiralty decided it was time
to take action against Zeebrugge, where it was believed the Germans had established a submarine
base. Two of the boats from our Dover patrol,
C-31 and *C-34,* were detailed for this special duty.
They were to take turn and turn about patrolling
just off the entrance to Zeebrugge, reporting all
they saw, and attacking any enemy vessels that
came their way.

To appreciate the importance of this work it is
well to recall the conditions that existed at that
time. The British Army in France was dependent
on a line of communications stretching across the
English Channel. The elaborate net defenses later
developed had not yet been established. A German
submarine and destroyer base at Zeebrugge, on the
very edge of the troop lane, was a menace the Brit-

ish Admiralty wished to have done away with. The
loss of the *Formidable* was a sufficient example of
what might happen.

The two submarines were to make reconnaissances and obtain all available information. They
were to try and estimate the strength of the enemy
squadrons operating from these bases. They were
to watch and report on their mine-laying and minesweeping activities, and a host of other things besides.

C-34 made two reconnaissances of the port and
returned with valuable information. *C-31* followed
after her return from the first trip and was never
heard of again. She probably located a mine field.
The plan to capture Zeebrugge, which would have
required the coöperation of land and sea forces,
was put off from time to time because of a difference of opinion between the British and French
high commands.

(2)

In another part of the North Sea C-boats were
being fitted out in the early months of 1915 for one
of the strangest adventures that ever befell sailors.

In compliance with the policy of unrestricted
submarine warfare, enemy boats were using our
fishing fleets for target practice while they engaged
in the peaceful pursuit of their business on the
Dogger Banks. The enemy justified this action by
claiming the right to starve Britain into submis-

sion, but the German crews went about their work in a different manner from that followed by the British submarine crews in the Sea of Marmora when faced with similar tasks. Our commanders always provided first for the safety of crews in boats they were forced to sink in the course of duty. The method employed by some of the German submarines was to come suddenly to the surface in the middle of a fishing fleet and sink by gunfire as many as possible before they could scatter and get out of range. A terrible loss of human life resulted.

Such indignation was aroused in the fishing ports that trawler crews offered to join the navy and sail as decoys to protect the other boats of the fishing fleets. This was tried for a time and one or two enemy submarines fell victims to their own frightfulness. They found that a harmless-looking fisherman was in reality an armed vessel with guns concealed under the fishing gear. It was this method of outwitting the enemy that gave birth to the idea of the Q-boats, or mystery ships, of the British Navy.

One cannot but admire the courage of the men who manned these decoy vessels for they were armed with guns so old and obsolete that other branches of the service had no use for them. So hard up were the troops in France for artillery that the navy had sent over all the guns it could possibly spare. Those fishermen had to go forth to

do battle with guns which were so inferior in type
to those the German submarines carried that it was
necessary for the decoy ship to manœuvre and flop
around, inviting attack, until they got so close to
the enemy submarine they could have heaved rocks
aboard her. As a matter of fact, some of these vessels actually carried lance bombs to be thrown by
hand. The patience and discipline necessary to succeed in an action of this kind were tremendous, and
yet these untrained fishermen won no small success.

In answer to appeals for protection from the
crews who manned the fishing fleet, there came a
suggestion from the officers who served in the
C-class submarines attached to H.M.S. *Vulcan*
based on Leith on the east coast of Scotland. The
plan arose from a simple discussion which turned
on the feasibility of a trawler's towing a submarine
submerged. If this were possible, the submarine
could lie doggo until an enemy submarine started
trouble. Once this was under way all the trawler
had to do was signal to the submerged boat, give
the position and range of the U-boat, slip the tow,
and let the waiting British boat do the rest. There
were many technical difficulties to overcome, but
the Admiralty decided to give the idea a try-out
and experiments were soon under way. The first
problem was to find out exactly how a submarine
would behave while being towed submerged. This
was proved possible. Further experiments were
conducted to perfect a towing gear that could be

slipped while the submarine remained submerged. This too was worked out in a satisfactory manner and the problem of connecting trawlers and subs by telephone was next tackled and solved. The idea originated in April, 1915, and by the beginning of June C-boats put to sea in tow of trawlers bound for the fishing banks.

Thus it was that, about three bells in the forenoon watch of June 23d, Lieutenant Taylor in command of submarine *C-24* heard his telephone bell ring, and on putting the receiver to his ear was informed by the officer on the trawler's bridge that a submarine had come to the surface fifteen hundred yards on the port beam. As previously arranged, the trawler altered course away from the enemy with the intention of decoying her past the position in which *C-24* would lurk, ready to fire. Then the trawler reported: "Submarine one thousand yards astern."

The trawler's job was completed. All she now had to do was stage a panic party, when her men would rush madly about the decks, man the boat, and abandon the trawler in a manner as little as possible like that of any trained naval crew.

While the surface ship was going ahead with her work, *C-24* was trying to slip her towing gear. It had been tested before she left port and found to work all right. But now, with the enemy in sight, the contraption wouldn't work. Fortunately the captain of the *Taranaki,* which was the name of

the trawler, was still at his post on the bridge, and
he lifted the telephone receiver in answer to *C-24's*
frantic ring and was informed of the trouble. He
was asked to slip his end of the tow. He did so.
The weight of 100 fathoms of 3½-inch wire and
the same length of 8-inch coir hawser and telephone wire suddenly dangling from her bows
caused *C-24* to try to turn a somersault and forced
her into a steep dive. She went down by the head.
By the time Lieutenant Taylor had compensated
his boat for the weight of towing gear, and got to
periscope depth again to take a look at the Fritz,
he discovered the wire had fouled his propeller.
Although everything possible had gone wrong,
Taylor managed his boat so well that she was in
her firing position within twenty-five minutes from
the time the first alarm had been given. He first
sighted the enemy's conning tower one thousand
yards away and, handicapped as he was, approached to within five hundred yards of her
without being seen, to make certain of his shot.
He got square on the enemy's beam and fired at
9:55 A.M. The torpedo struck fair amidships and
U-40 went on her last crash dive, never more to
sink fishing vessels. Her captain and one petty officer were the only survivors. It was reported that
they remarked that they had been victims of a dirty
trick.

Lieutenant Commander Edwards who commanded the trawler *Taranaki* tersely reported the incident:

"9:30 A.M., June 23d: Enemy submarine rose and fired a shot across my bows from 200 yards' range. Shell burst 20 yards ahead. Informed *C-24* by telephone. 9:45: Slipped *Taranaki's* end of tow, as *C-24's* slip had jammed. Got boat out to stimulate abandon ship and panic. Saw *C-24's* periscope pass, attacking. 9:55: Observed torpedo run and explode under conning tower of enemy. An officer and petty officer only survivors."

Sixty-six words to describe one of the most dramatic incidents of the whole war. Two words to each minute of nerve-racking suspense.

What happened in the C-boat? Each man of her crew, all youngsters at the game of submarine warfare, undoubtedly set out on the end of those towing hawsers like a bridegroom to his wedding.

For days they drifted around secretly attached to a vessel which looked no different from the others employed in gathering the harvest of the sea. As night fell and darkness shut out the horizon, the trawler with its strange tow would escape for a while from the fishing fleet and the old C-boat would come to the surface and charge her batteries. Thus day after day dragged monotonously along, sixteen to eighteen hours submerged out of every twenty-four hours. The men were seeing nothing, doing nothing, except wait for the tinkle of the telephone bell which would notify

them that an enemy was in sight. Imagine then the
first glorious thrill they experienced when, in answer to a summons on the phone, their youthful
commander, Lieutenant Taylor, told them that an
enemy submarine had been sighted. Here was what
they had hoped for. Here was an opportunity to
do something. Then from the pinnacle of hope
they were dashed to the depths of despair. The men
who had rushed for'ard to release the towing gear
on their officer's order yelled through the hollow
shell of the boat. "The damn thing won't work, sir.
We can't slip the tow."

Leaving the control room, after instructing the
men on the hydroplanes to keep the boat at twenty
feet, the captain rushed for'ard to try to slip the
towing gear himself. It had worked all right during the trials in port. What could the trouble be
now? They couldn't come to the surface with the
enemy in sight; they couldn't manœuvre the boat
with a trawler hold of the bow. They stood and
cursed their luck. What was going on above them?
Was Fritz shelling the fleet they were supposed to
protect? They could hear nothing. There was but
one thing to do and the effect of that could only
be imagined. Taylor hesitated a moment, and then
called the trawler captain on the phone. "My end
is jammed. I can't slip the tow. You slip your end."

Back in the control room he waited for what he
knew must surely happen. He warned the men and
stood ready to act. Slowly at first, then more rap-

idly, the submarine took an angle by the head. She almost stood on her head and went into a nose dive as the weight of two heavy towing lines and fathoms of telephone wire dangled from her bows. "Flood the after tanks. Blow the for'ard ones. Blow your main ballast tanks." Bracing themselves against the angle of the boat, the men obeyed the orders, leaving everything to the judgment of the mere boy who commanded them, willing to take any risk he took.

Think what the satisfaction must have been when they were able to offset the weight of the dragging tow ropes and telephone cable by flooding water into the after tanks and blowing it out of the for'ard ones; then picture their chagrin at the moment they thought they had overcome all these difficulties when they discovered their propellers were fouled. The towing gear, flowing astern like long tresses, had tangled itself around the propellers and brought the motors up all standing with a shock. Picture the determination which caused the youth who commanded that C-boat to order the motors driven at full speed that they might with luck propel her the last few hundred yards essential to the success of the attack, even though they burned themselves out or the wires chewed through the propeller shaft.

This is what happened in *C-24* that midsummer morning. What satisfaction the crew felt when, after waiting that seeming eternity experienced by

the crews of all submarines between the time the
torpedo leaves the tube and the moment it ought to
explode, they felt the shock and concussion and
knew they had avenged some hundreds of men
who at their peaceful calling had been sent to their
deaths suddenly and without warning.

(3)

Less than one month later, on July 20th, at 7:55
A. M., as half the crew of *C-27* were finishing their
breakfast prior to relieving their mates at eight
bells, Lieutenant Commander Dobson, with whom
I later served in another flotilla, heard his telephone tinkle. Lieutenant Cantlie, commanding the
trawler *Princess Louise,* informed him that a Fritz
had bobbed to the surface about two thousand
yards away, on the port bow. He advised Dobson
against slipping the tow just at that moment and
then the telephone broke down.

It was one of the things that would happen in
submarines. Just at the moment we most needed
everything to work smoothly, something would go
wrong. If we were on the surface at night and it
was necessary to use the arc light to flash a challenge or reply that meant all the difference between death and safety, the fuse would blow out.
If we were making an attack and were bucking a
broken sea and using the utmost skill to avoid
breaking surface, the hydroplanes would likely
jam, or, if we had succeeded in firing our fish, they

would break surface with a rush and a roar or
develop a gyro failure, and, instead of heading for
the enemy, start chasing circles around the boat
from which they had been fired. But all these
things were part of the game. We accepted them
like salt with our meals. Dobson proceeded to get
along without the use of the telephone.

Hearing shells explode in the water above him,
he decided to slip the towing gear and edge up to
the surface for a peep. At eighteen feet he put the
tip of his periscope above water. He had to turn
quickly to starboard to avoid crashing into his
escort and then took another peep and located the
enemy submarine which was shelling the fishing
boats and the escort. The trawler had a concealed
gun but did not use it. Her job was to give the
C-boat first chance because a torpedo below the
waterline was a surer way of sending the U-boat
to the bottom than by shelling her with a small
gun.

Dobson worked his way to within five hundred
yards of the enemy. She was sitting on the surface,
blazing away at the fishing fleet. At eight-twelve,
seventeen minutes from the time she was first
sighted, *C-27* fired her fish. Just as she did, the
Fritz kicked ahead with her engines and the torpedo missed astern.

Dobson had seen all this through his periscope.
Allowing a little more deflection, he let go a second torpedo with better results. It exploded just

abaft the conning tower. He immediately blew his tanks and went over to the spot where the boat had disappeared, and was able to rescue seven of her crew, the captain, two officers, and four other ratings, most of whom had been manning the guns.

The stunt over, the crew of the submarine finished their interrupted meal, and Lieutenant Cantlie aboard the trawler compiled another masterpiece of literary economy:

"7:55 A. M., July 20th: Sighted hostile submarine three points on port bow, distance 2,500 yards. Informed *C-27* and told her not to slip yet. Hostile submarine steaming across my bows. 7:56: Enemy opened fire. Apparently trying to hit trawler. Telephone to *C-27* broke down. 8:03: Tow slipped. Enemy fired seven shots altogether. Employed crew rushing about, lowering boat and acting as if in a panic. 8:10: Observed *C-27's* periscope on starboard quarter attacking enemy. 8:12: Observed *C-27* fire a torpedo which missed astern. Cleared away gun for action. Enemy opened fire again and commenced turning to port. I opened fire with my starboard gun and hoisted white ensign at main. At the same moment second torpedo hit just abaft enemy's conning tower. Column of water and smoke rose about 80 feet high. As it cleared away about 30 feet of the bow of the submarine could be seen."

That is all. It was enough. *U-23* went down stern first to join her consort *U-40*.

These two actions had a great moral effect on the crews of enemy submarines. Our fishing boats were not interfered with again until well on in 1916. There is little doubt that the mysterious loss of two boats sent out within a month of each other on what might be considered a safe mission caused the enemy to abandon the campaign against fishing boats. The Germans undoubtedly guessed that some strangely potent method of dealing with submarines had been evolved, and until they discovered what the method was they considered it the better part of valour to lay off fishing fleets.

It was unfortunate for the fishing fleets that the enemy did not remain in ignorance for the duration of the war, but the survivors of the two U-boats were allowed to mingle in the prison camp with civilian prisoners who were waiting to be repatriated and in that manner the true story of *U-23* and *U-40* became known in Germany. With this knowledge the enemy once more turned his attention to our fishing fleets in the middle of 1916. Again our C-boats undertook the hazardous patrols, but the Germans were forewarned, and were able to offset the effectiveness of this method of attack. After the unfortunate sinking of Lieutenant Schofield's boat, *C-29,* with the loss of all hands, when she struck a mine while being towed off the Humber on August 29, 1916, the scheme was abandoned.

CHAPTER ELEVEN

My own introduction to the Trade came only after months of waiting. When war broke out I was nineteen years of age, serving as fourth officer of the S. S. *Sizergh Castle* trading between Antwerp and the ports of South America. We were in Buenos Aires. It will be remembered how everyone at that time thought the war would last only a few months, and how Britishers the world over flocked home to England to make certain of a ringside seat at the greatest show ever staged by an imbecile humanity. I had been four years at sea; I left the merchant ship to hurry home and join the navy. Before I reached home the British and German navies had already established a stalemate.

On my way down to Royal Naval Barracks at

Devonport, shortly after reaching England, I met Lieutenant Max Horton, the captain of submarine *E-9*. Her doings were already the talk of the younger naval men who wanted action. I first saw Horton in a tram car. He was a young man, but already the breast of his jacket was a beribboned proof of high adventure. I remember that he lit one cigarette from the butt of the other, and tapped a steady light tattoo with his fingers on the window sill of the tram. I spoke to him; probably the bravest thing I did during the whole war. From then on I worked to get in submarines.

It was not easy. My first application was turned down. The only officers of the Royal Naval Reserve needed were those qualified as navigators. I was too young; I had not had the necessary experience. Disappointed, I was forced to go into the big ships.

While serving on H. M. S. *Virginian,* one of the ships of the 10th Cruiser Squadron, I was able to establish my abilities as a navigator. I succeeded in getting Commander Wilding, R.N., to recommend me. The recommendation went through at last and January, 1917, found me on my way to Harwich, the principal submarine base and known, truthfully enough, as "the Graveyard of the Fleet." After a short period awaiting appointment I was sent up to Blyth as navigating officer to H. M. Submarine *G-6*.

I found myself in company with many officers

and men who had achieved fine records as submarine officers. Attached to the submarine depot ship *Titania* were twelve overseas submarines based on Blyth. *G-1* to *G6* and *J-1* to *J-6*. Two C-class boats also operated from this base, but they were principally engaged in coastal patrol duties. These submarines, with the exception of the C-boats, were all new, modern boats built for overseas patrols. They were commanded and manned by officers and men who had nearly all seen service in the Dardanelles or the Baltic. Among the officers attached to the flotilla when I joined were Commander Max Horton, D.S.O. and bar, etc., *J-6*; Commander Boyle, V.C., etc., *J-5*; Commander Goodhart. D.S.O.; Commander Laurence, D.S.O.; Commander Ramsey, and Sir Edward Carson's son, who was in command of one of the C-boats.

The officer I relieved in submarine *G-6* was Lieutenant Howell-Price, D.S.C., R.N.R. He had been decorated when the ship he was on, previous to joining submarines, fought and sank the German raider *Greif*. At that time he was serving in the 10th Cruiser Squadron, I think on the *Almanzora*. I remember meeting him several times during the early part of 1916 when I was serving on H. M. S. *Virginian* of the same squadron. Price was a very capable officer and had taken a great interest in the mechanical part of submarines as well as in their navigation. He had taken *G-6* on a voyage to north Russia where she patrolled the waters of

the Arctic looking for enemy mine layers reported
to be operating off Archangel. He had been recom-
mended for promotion to first lieutenant. After
taking his course at Fort Blockhouse he was appointed to *C-3* as first lieutenant and the world
knows how he assisted his youthful captain, Lieutenant Sandford, in blowing up the viaduct which
connected the Mole in that glorious epic known as
the Raid on Zeebrugge. The first lieutenant of
G-6 was Lieutenant Holland-Pryor, "Tin-ribs" we
called him, and Lieutenant C. Coltart was in command.

Lieutenant Price took me over the boat and introduced me to my duties and to those members
of the crew, particularly the electricians, who
would help me when any of the electrical instruments went out of order. I met also the signal rating, "Nobby" Clark, one of the most efficient and
willing men I ever met, who performed the rôles
of signal rating, officers' mess steward, and general
handy man.

The atmosphere in the ward room of the depot
ship was like that of a big happy family. During
the afternoons, when the boats had been groomed
after their return from patrol, we played games—
football, rugger, tennis, or cricket—depending on
the season of the year—and in the evenings, cards.
We sang an extraordinary amount and drank with
normal enthusiasm. The depot was situated where,
in peace time, the fishing boats had landed their

catches, and the fish market was fitted up as a rec-
reation room, with billiard tables and other means
of entertainment.

Among other officers in the Blyth flotilla were
Lieutenant Blair, R.N.R., who navigated Scott's
ship on his expedition to the South Pole, Commander Ramsey, a relative of the officer who married Princess Patricia, and many others who had
interesting careers both in and out of the service.

When I joined *G-6* she had just returned from
patrol. Previous to that she was one of the three
submarines sent up to Alexandrovsk in north Russia. They left about the middle of October, 1916.
We heard much of the long and wonderful trips of
German U-boats but I soon learned that our own
boats had made remarkable journeys. The voyage
of the G-boats up to the Murmansk coast, the voyage of the E-boats into the Sea of Marmora and
into the Baltic, the voyages of the H-boats from
Halifax across the Atlantic were all equal to, and
most of them performed previous to, the Atlantic
voyages made by those enemy submarines to which
the world's press gave such prominence.

The G-boats were very similar to the E-boats
except that they had double hulls. It was thought
that these might prove a protection against attack
by the newfangled depth charges, and even against
gunfire.

They are seven feet longer than an E-boat and
displace about two hundred tons more when sub-

merged. They are armed with five torpedo tubes
—two beam and two bow tubes, each firing
eighteen-inch torpedoes, and one twenty-one-inch
tube in the stern. In addition to their torpedo
armament they carry two three-inch Q. F. guns,
mounted fore and aft of the conning tower. The inside arrangement of these boats is in some ways a
slight improvement on the E-boats.

The for'ard compartment is a space about thirty
feet long and about sixteen feet wide. The entire
width of a G-boat allowing for its double hull is
twenty-two feet, eight inches. Right for'ard in the
bows are the two torpedo tubes. To one side of
them are the air cylinders containing the compressed air for firing the torpedoes out of the tubes.
At the sides of the boat in brackets are the spare
torpedoes. Behind them is the electric cooking
stove which the officers use, and a toilet.

A hatch opens on to the for'ard deck of the boat
from the for'ard compartment. The torpedoes for
the for'ard tubes are loaded into the boat through
this hatch, which also provides a quick way of
passing up ammunition to the for'ard gun, weather
permitting.

The for'ard compartment is separated from the
control room, which is the next compartment aft,
by a watertight bulkhead. A watertight door gives
access from one to the other. The control room is
the heart or the brains of the boat. From it the officers direct everything. It contains the steering

gear and hydroplane gears, or horizontal rudders, which steer the boat up or down when under water and keep her at the required depth.

The periscopes are also situated here, together with all valves controlling the flooding or empty-ing of the various trimming and ballast tanks. The main electrical switchboard is also located in the control room, as well as the nautical instruments, the Sperry Gyroscopic Compass, the log, the safe in which the confidential code books and charts are stored, and so forth.

Tucked away on each side of the compartment at the for'ard end are the bunks in which the cap-tain and first lieutenant of the boat sleep. Under the bunks are chart drawers and food lockers. The dining table, also used as a chart table, pulls out from under the starboard bunk. The bottom drawer under the starboard bunk is intended by those who designed the boat to act as a bed for the navigator or spare officer. As the space between the two bunks leading into the for'ard compart-ment is about four feet wide, the idea of the lower drawer as a bed is not what could be called a howl-ing success. Every time a man has to pass from the control room into the for'ard compartment he has to climb over the officer sleeping in it.

To enter the conning tower from the control room an iron ladder leads upward through a hatch into a chamber called the lower conning tower. This compartment is only a few feet in diameter.

From there another ladder leads out on to the conning-tower deck.

The periscopes pass from the control room through the conning tower, in a sleeve called the periscope standard. The chamber separating the upper conning tower from the control room could be damaged by shell fire or collision without endangering the boat, as long as the lower hatch was not damaged. Passing from the control room aft, you go through another watertight door and enter a compartment in which the crew has its mess tables and cooking stove. Running athwart ship are the two beam torpedo tubes. Just abaft them and on the starboard side is the wireless cabinet.

The next compartment aft, also equipped with a watertight door and bulkhead, is the engine room. On each side of this space are installed the two Diesel engines which propel the boat while on the surface. A passage leads down the middle of the engine room between the engines to the after compartment where most of the crew find space to sleep. The motors, which propel the boat when submerged, are also located there.

Aft as far as you can go is the twenty-one-inch torpedo tube. Jammed into this compartment also are the dynamos, which charge the batteries when the submarine is running on the surface. The batteries themselves are stowed under the decks or floors of the control room and centre compartments.

Beneath the engine-room floor are situated the fuel tanks, and beneath the floors of the other compartments are the ballast tanks which are flooded or emptied to make the boat sink or rise. At either end of the submarine are the trimming tanks. These tanks are connected with each other by a pipe line, and it is possible to blow water either way to regulate the trim of the boat when submerged. To dive, water is let into the ballast tanks, causing her to sink beneath the surface. This accomplished, the water in the tanks is juggled by pumping or blowing a little out, or letting a little more in, until the submarine is in what is called neutral buoyancy. Then the water in the fore and aft trimming tanks is juggled to give the boat the same weight at both ends. This done, it is very easy for the men at the hydroplanes to keep her at any depth required. Of course, consumption of fuel and stores has to be considered and compensated for, and difficulty is often experienced in controlling the diving trim of the boat when patrolling in water where there are frequent changes in density.

In addition to the details already noted there are the high- and low-pressure air systems. These consist of a number of cylinders located in various parts of the boat which contain compressed air. Each is charged to a pressure of 3,000 lbs. to the square inch. This pressure is of course too great for ordinary use, so the air is passed into a reducing chamber where it is kept ready for use till required.

Each boat carries its own air compressor, ventilating pumps, emergency lighting system, air purifier, and a hundred and one other gadgets too numerous to mention. Most of the vital equipment can be operated either by electricity or by hand, and many of the boats have hydraulic equipment as well.

A submarine has two sets of compasses. The magnetic and the Sperry Gyroscopic Compass. The magnetic is unreliable, due to the influence of the vast amount of electrical equipment in the boat. The Gyro compasses are not supposed to be influenced by anything. They are operated on the theory that a gyro, or wheel, revolved in space at 6,800 revolutions per minute, will take up its position at right angles to the earth's axis, and thus give you the true north and south points.

It will when the sea is calm. But when the winds blow, and the sea gets rough, and the boat begins to pitch and toss about, the Gyro seems to think that there is no reason why it should remain the only sober thing in the boat. Generally it begins to "go off" or "wander," as we called it. When it does a bell rings. And the bell rings whether the navigator is asleep or awake, usually when he is asleep. It is then up to him to locate the trouble and correct it. Often it goes off because a little speck of dirt has got into its delicate mechanism, or a speck of dust is bridging the gold and silver contacts. They are awfully fussy creatures, harder to manage and understand than a woman. We called them in the service "the navigator's nightmare."

To assist in navigation, the pilot has also an electrical log. It never worked when it was most required. That was when we were doing a submerged patrol at a very slow speed. The log does not register correctly below three knots. There is also a chronometer watch. These kept really good time if they did not become magnetized. We also carried sextants, charts, etc.

A submarine, in short, is intricate, complicated, and temperamental: a triumph of mechanical ingenuity and discomfort.

(2)

Our first patrol took us to a position off Horn's Reef. To reach there we had to navigate through the protective mine fields off our own coasts and around No. 1 mined area in the centre of the North Sea and then run to our patrol position during the hours of darkness. We were to attack enemy submarines homeward or outward bound, to watch for and report the movements of enemy ships, and to attack any single ships we might see, or squadrons which might be sighted making toward their bases.

We were hardly straightened away on the course which would take us to the northern edge of No. 1

mined area when I sighted something that looked like a large buoy of the type used for marking channels.

The sea was glassy and it was one of those days when sea and sky merge into each other without any line of demarkation. The whole dome of heaven and the vast expanse of sea beneath it were a dead, uninterrupted pall of steely gray. The object we had sighted was not more than two thousand yards away, and only a shade darker than its surroundings.

The moment I put the binoculars to my eyes I recognized the object ahead to be a submarine. I reported the fact to Coltart. He glanced through his glasses and then pressed the button for a crash dive. The Klaxton horns clattered through the boat. The engines stopped.

"Get down quick. Tell the first lieutenant to steady her at twenty-four feet, and flood the bow tubes," Coltart ordered.

I dropped down into the control room. Coltart was close behind me and we were at sixty feet by the depth gauge before I realized we were even submerged. Holland-Pryor brought her back up to twenty-four feet and trimmed her so the men could control her depth easily with the hydroplanes. Coltart anxiously waited for the periscope to show above surface. When it did he was just in time to see the top of the enemy's conning tower dip beneath the waves. Nothing could have been more exasperating.

We hung around for more than an hour, watching for any reappearance of the enemy. We heard him on our hydrophones, but dusk fell without his coming to the surface, and when it was too dark to see him we blew our tanks and proceeded to our patrol position.

The weather during the whole of that first patrol was abominable. It blew big guns nearly all the time and it was also beastly cold. We sighted nothing but fishing vessels and not many of these until after the weather improved. I think I got sights four times during the whole of the ten days we were actually on patrol, and I learned what it meant to navigate "by guess and by God."

The last day of our patrol we went to action stations in a hurry. Pryor, keeping the periscope watch, sighted what he took to be another Fritz. It turned out to be the nearest of a fleet of fishing vessels. They drifted right over our position, and about eight bells during the afternoon watch we accidentally broke surface right in the middle of them. The crews of the nearest vessels commenced to abandon ship with a sincerity that would have made some of our own Q-boat panic parties green with envy. Coltart came to the surface and told them to go back to their boats. The captain of the nearest boat gave us ten fine codfish and we passed him a bottle of rum.

We dived again and headed toward the outer limits of our patrol. We came to the surface during the second dog watch, and while keeping the conning-tower watch that evening I saw for myself just how thick mines were in the North Sea.

In two hours I saw more than a dozen mines floating on the surface, evidently broken adrift from their mooring by the heavy weather. We passed up a couple of rifles and indulged in a little target practice. Most of the mines sank as soon as bullets perforated the outer casing, but in one instance the bullet hit one of the horns and the whole works blew skyward. There was a dull flash and a roar, and a heavy thick black smoke shot into the air to a height of around two hundred feet, amply demonstrating the deadly power each mine contained. I couldn't keep from thinking about mines which might not have broken adrift and were still out of sight.

I was beastly sick most of the trip. The smell of the oil, the close atmosphere of the boat, and the motion while on the surface at night keeping watch all combined to give my stomach an ordeal it had never experienced before. I had been at sea more than seven years before I went into submarines, but I never met anything to equal the motion of a submarine while on the surface in a storm. Tin-ribs was no better off than myself. He was violently sick most of the trip, as were most of the crew. Tin-ribs was so called because he had had an operation and a silver tube had replaced some internal part of his anatomy. He served from the beginning to the end of the war in submarines, and only those who have served with him knew how he suffered when the weather was bad and he had frequent vomiting spells. Yet he wouldn't complain and wouldn't quit. He was made of the same stuff as all the rest.

Only those who have themselves actually experienced the horrors of seasickness can have any conception of the agony men who served in submarines suffered when they were sick as the result of a combination of bad weather, foul air, improper food, and breathing an atmosphere saturated with the fumes of crude oil and gassing batteries. Imagine trying to work out problems in navigation when your stomach was in such revolt that you worked with a pail beside you and cold clammy sweat, trickling down from your forehead and dripping off the end of your chin, smeared the pages of the work book in which you tried to figure. The greatest agony was that one couldn't always be sick. We had to use every ounce of will power to get on our feet and do our work.

We headed for home on the surface. During the night the weather mended and at dawn I got the first real sights since we had left the base—double-altitude star sights—and was happy in as much as I felt sure of making a good landfall. After I had worked them out I wasn't so happy. The position they gave me was dead centre of No. 1 mined area. Bad weather and lack of sights had caused us to drift many miles out of our position. As we were equi-distant from all sides of the area, I set a straight course for home. I'm not foolish enough to try and describe my feelings until we had passed clear of the field. I remember saying to myself, "Well, the damn things are laid at least a hundred yards apart, perhaps more, and the chances are all in our favour." In my heart I didn't think they were.

At dawn we were just about in the same position as when we sighted the submarine on our outward trip.

A large steamer was bearing sharp on our starboard bow as the sun showed over the eastern horizon. She was steering so she would pass close ahead of us. I altered course a little to go well clear of her stern, and as I did so a trawler which was acting as her escort, and which had kept snug alongside her the moment she had reported sighting us, opened fire on us as we came into view around her stern. She only fired one round. That was enough for my comfort. The whiz of the shell lifted some of our caps off as it passed over us. The trawler saw our marks then and stopped firing. These incidents were all too common for comfort in the submarine service. I was fired on at least eight times by our own ships before the end of the war, and on each occasion it was when making port or leaving a home port. I suppose if our surface boats had been less aggressive they would have sunk fewer enemy submarines.

(3)

We were moored alongside the depot ship in time to have a hot bath before breakfast. That bath and all the others I had after returning from fourteen days' patrol were the finest things I ever enjoyed in my life. Black from oil fumes, greasy, uncomfortable, and tired, to flop into a hot bath and lie in plenty of changes of water and soak till all the dirt and tiredness had oozed out was only a degree removed from sheer heaven.

What was true of one trip was true of most of the others, except for weather conditions. There was always enough excitement to remind you that there was a war on and that the trips you made were no pleasure cruises.

The hot summer weather was most trying. If you were in an area where there was any other craft at all it meant long tedious dives. You could not afford to allow even innocent neutral fishermen to sight you because they would talk when they returned to port with their catch. Once your position was known you might as well pack up and go home. To prevent being seen meant diving during the summer months from eighteen to twenty hours out of every twenty-four.

After five or six hours' diving the air in the boat

would not contain sufficient oxygen to support a lighted match. If you struck one it would simply flicker and go out. I don't know where the idea originated that submarines carried supplies of oxygen, but none of the four different classes of boat I served in carried any. We did use "purifiers," a sort of box arrangement containing lime. The air in the boat was sucked into the purifier and passed out back into the boat again, supposedly cleansed of its impurities.

During the long dives the men who were not actually on duty would rest most of the time. The officer on watch had the most trying time for he had to keep his eye glued to the rubber eyepiece of the periscope. Through a periscope the range of vision is limited to a circle of water the extent of which depends on the height the top of the periscope is above the water. The height of the periscope is limited by the condition of the sea. In rough weather the boat has to be kept deeper— to retain control of her while diving, and to prevent her from breaking surface—than is necessary in fine weather with a calm sea.

Under ideal weather conditions it was possible to have eight feet or more of stick out of water and thus have a range of vision of from three to four miles. In rough weather, when the boat was bumping badly, we would be lucky to have a range of vision of more than one or one and a half miles. This being the case, it can be readily understood

why an officer had to keep his eye almost constantly
at the periscope. If he didn't, an enemy vessel
might pass the arc of his range of vision when he
wasn't looking. A vessel two miles away could appear in and pass out of the range of the periscope
in one minute or even less. It was also essential
to get the earliest possible warning of an approaching enemy, because a minute of time meant all the
difference between "getting in your attack" and
"failing to get it in." Ships were not always sighted
heading in the direction which would bring them
within range. Most often, when an enemy or a
possible enemy was sighted, it was necessary to
chase off after her and try to intercept her. To get
there the motors had to be driven at full speed,
and when that happened the batteries did not last
more than a couple of hours.

These were the circumstances under which *G-6*
attacked the only enemy surface ship we sighted
under conditions favourable to attack while on patrol. We were patrolling in the waters at the entrance to the Baltic when Holland-Pryor sighted
a three-funnelled cruiser. She was hull down with
masts and funnels alone showing when he first
picked her up. By the space which appeared between her funnels and masts we knew that she was
steering a parallel course almost to our own. We
were far from sure of her identity at first. Once
during the patrol we had been ordered to get out of
the way of our light cruisers and destroyers which

were making one of their periodical sweeps, and
the silhouette of the ship sighted looked very much
like that of some of our own light cruisers.

We went at full speed, however, and steered at
an angle which would have brought us to within
about three thousand yards of her. This was the
nearest we could hope to get if she continued her
course and speed. Suddenly she altered course and
headed in a direction which would bring her directly past us at an estimated range of about one
thousand yards. I was at the plotting table working out, from the information and bearings the
captain had passed me, the enemy's course and
speed, and checking up Coltart's mental estimates.
The men stood by, outwardly calm, but inwardly
thrilled with the possibility of what was about to
happen. Coltart was very careful with his periscope now. He showed just the tip and then lowered it the moment he saw everything was O. K.

He had slowed down the motors. All we had to
do was wait a minute more. By this time the cruiser
would pass straight across our bows within one
thousand yards of us. We had been able to figure
out her speed from a series of bearings taken while
we were steaming on parallel courses. Both bow
tubes were flooded and the torpedoes ready. Nothing could have worked out better from our point of
view.

Nobby Clark had already begun to figure out
how he was going to spend his blood money.

Glancing at his watch, Coltart gave the order, "Raise periscope slowly." He crouched down and raised himself with his eye glued to the periscope eyepiece and the instrument trained in the direction the enemy should bear by this time.

All hands stopped breathing. I know I felt that to breathe or move might warn the enemy. Everyone had his eyes on Coltart's face. All watched him, trying by some sort of mental telepathy to see what he could see. They saw him start to move the periscope more and more. They instinctively knew something was wrong. Finally he spoke: "Raise periscope." Up shot the instrument to its full height. The enemy had again altered course directly away from us. It was worse than useless to fire at her.

CHAPTER TWELVE

Bᴌɪɴᴅ chance seems to have been the only govern-
ing factor in the life of the submarine. Max Horton served with submersibles from the very outbreak of hostilities. He made some of the most
dangerous trips every undertaken in under-water
craft, and never turned down an opportunity to
attack the enemy. Yet he is alive to-day. But there
seems no reason why he should not be among those
33 per cent. of the personnel of the submarine service who are remembered by the beautiful monu-
ment erected on the Thames Embankment.

When I left the Blyth flotilla in November,
1917, Horton was still captain of *J-6*. I met him
again while I was down at Portsmouth getting the
secret and confidential documents and papers for

Submarine *R-12*. She was being built in Liverpool and I had been appointed her navigator. Horton was then in command of the huge submersible
M-1. This submarine was armed with a twelve-
inch gun in addition to her torpedo tubes. Lieutenant McKenzie, the first officer of the new M-
boat, had taken his first trip overseas with me in
Submarine *G-6* early in 1917. He had accompanied us then just for the experience. We were
glad to meet each other again and I was invited to
look over the new wonder ship and have tea on
board. It must have been about the very time we
were sitting around the mess table sipping our tea
and talking over the extraordinary luck of the
Blyth flotilla that the horrible drama which ended
the career of *J-6* was being enacted in the cold
gray mists of the North Sea off Blyth.

It was eleven years later before I heard the story
of how *J-6* met her end. In Toronto one evening,
while visiting the home of an ex-naval officer to
discuss certain of the incidents related in this book,
I found myself talking to one of the very men who
had taken part in the most tragic incident of the
British Submarine Service.

He has given me permission to tell the story as
he told it to me, with the request that neither his
name nor the name of his commanding officer be
used. His story follows. There is no need to comment on it save perhaps to repeat his own comment

that nothing he has ever heard illustrates better the vicious stupidity of war.

"I was serving in a Q-boat," he said, "commanded by an officer who had a distinguished service record. He had been awarded the D. S. O. and bar, the D. S. C. and bar, and other decorations. Many thought he should have been given the V. C. The Q-boat was an old topsail schooner which had been turned into a first-class mystery ship at considerable expense. When the officer was given command of the newest thing in anti-submarine warfare he felt that a real honour had been conferred on him and the crew was equally pleased to have the opportunity of serving on such a ship and under such a captain. I only mention these facts to show that he was anything but a nervous or inexperienced officer.

"We left the Firth of Forth and proceeded south, bound for the English Channel. We had received plenty of reports that enemy submarines were operating in the vicinity of Blyth. It was a peculiar kind of day—little wind, and sea and sky seemed to blend together. It was almost impossible to define the horizon. About four bells in the forenoon watch we went to action stations. A large submarine had been sighted about twenty-five hundred yards away. We studied the submarine carefully through our glasses and recognized her as one of our own K-class. We exchanged signals and proceeded on our way. We had only gone a few

miles farther on our course when we sighted another submarine and the men again closed up at
their action stations. Once more it proved to be one
of our own submarines.

"About eight bells in the afternoon the sea was
an unbroken expanse of purplish gray reflecting a
gray sky. The clouds were low. Smoke left by passing steamers clung strangely to the water. Banks
of mist formed and drifted about us. One moment
we had fair visibility, the next we couldn't see
more than a few hundred yards away.

"The watch was just about to change when we
sighted a third submarine. She was steering so that
she would pass us close on our starboard beam.
The men were ordered to their stations again and
crouched concealed near their camouflaged guns.
As the sub drew close I could distinctly hear a
whisper pass along the line of anxiously waiting
men:

"'U-6.' . . . 'U-6.' . . . 'U-6.' . . . 'It's a Fritz!' "

"I saw the boat and her markings plainly. I cannot tell what it was that hung over the conning
tower and completed the loop of the J making it
look like a U, but I was as convinced as any of
the men that it was a German U-boat. We thought
she was looking us over prior to sending us to the
bottom. Our captain was equally convinced that
it was an enemy vessel. He gave the order to break
the white ensign and open fire.

"There was not enough breeze to blow the flag

out of its folds. Just before the first gun fired I noticed that the submarine was also flying a flag, but it hung straight up and down from the masthead. If it had blown clean out I doubt very much if it would have made any difference. The commander had already lost one U-boat because he held his fire when she showed the white ensign.

"The moment the white ensign broke at our mast head the screens hiding our armament dropped down and the guns opened up in independent fire. We were practically at point-blank range. On the conning tower of the submarine stood an officer and a man. The man was about to lift a rifle to his shoulder to fire a recognition signal. The very first shell we fired broke his arms and killed the officer. The second pierced the submarine about the waterline just under the conning tower. We heard afterward that this shell exploded in the control room, completely wrecking it, and that the officer in charge ordered the fore and aft watertight bulkhead doors closed to prevent any other compartments filling. The submarine was still under way and by this time was on our quarter where our big four-inch gun could bear. The first shell from this gun was also a direct hit. Then we saw the after hatch open and an officer scramble on deck frantically waving what appeared to be a white tablecloth.

"We ceased fire, but immediately we did so the submarine altered course and headed into a fog bank. We opened fire again and shelled her until she was lost to sight in the mist. Just as she disappeared into the fog we saw her signalling HELP . . . HELP . . . HELP on her arc lamp.

"Satisfied that she was badly hit, but furious to think she had escaped us before we had the satisfaction of knowing she had actually sunk, we cursed the fog that hid her from us.

"In the meantime we had got our auxiliary engines working and changed course to head toward the direction in which the submarine had disappeared. Then the fog lifted again, just as the curtain rises on a new act of a play.

"The submarine was dead ahead of us. Her bows were high in the air. Part of her conning tower was just out of water. She had launched her small collapsible boat and we could see a number of men in the water struggling to keep afloat. We headed toward them and the small boat came alongside. The first thing I noticed was the marking 'H. M. Submarines' on the bands of the men's hats. We were absolutely stunned. We had sunk a British submarine by mistaking the 'J' for a 'U.' On their part, the submarine crew had been equally certain that they had run into an enemy Q-boat or raider making for the trade routes, and I can remember a big red-headed chap who was badly wounded shouting to us from the boat as he recognized us as British: 'Come on you fellows. Hurry up. They are your own men. Give them a hand.'

"That fellow's shout gave us strength to pick up the big boat which we ordinarily put over the side with tackle. The submarine's crew had scrambled aboard and with their help all hands lifted up the boat, dropped it overboard, and jumped after it.

"We pulled over to the sinking men. One man was holding up his commanding officer. He yelled 'Come and help me save Mr. ——' Others were sinking for the third time. We dived in after them and rescued all we could. Some we took out of the water were too far gone, however, and although we worked over them for hours after we got them on board, they died. We were able to save the lives of about fifteen out of her crew of thirty-four. We sent a signal to Blyth to say we were making for there with the survivors of *J-6* aboard.

"I'll never forget entering the port from which the J-boats operated. As we rounded the pier and worked our way into the basin where the depot ship and the other submarines were moored we could see the people—the wives and families of the crew of the ill-fated *J-6*—lined up gazing with anxious eyes to see if those dear to them were among the survivors.

"A court of inquiry was ordered and sat next day. We were exonerated from all blame. In fact our gun crews were congratulated on their wonderful gunnery. But the thing that stands out in my memory most is the fact that when my captain and I left the room in which the court sat, the sur-

vivors of *J-6* who had attended to give evidence
sprang smartly to attention and saluted us. A wonderful example of training and discipline, I have
always thought. They were true sportsmen. What
had happened was due to the risks of the game. It
was the war."

(2)

There were many other similar incidents experienced by crews of submarines during the war. I
myself when serving in *G-6* only narrowly missed
meeting the same fate at the hands of an American
destroyer which mistook us for a Fritz and was so
well satisfied that she had sunk us that she reported
to the officer commanding the naval base at Plymouth: "Attacked and sank enemy submarine in
position . . . Saw shells register direct hits. Felt
shock as we passed over her intending to ram.
Dropped depth charges in position in which she
disappeared."

Thank heavens the report was exaggerated, for
this is what actually happened:

We were stationed in Bantry Bay on the southwest coast of Ireland in the early part of December, 1917. Our duties consisted in patrolling the
western approaches of the English Channel and
hunting the German submarines which forever
lurked about the shipping lanes waiting to attack
the Allied merchantmen bound for the Channel
ports.

The convoy system had been generally adopted and the method of procedure usually followed was for ships bound for British ports to arrive at a given rendezvous on a certain date. This rendezvous would be in the vicinity of the English Channel and the ships when they met would be escorted into port by cruisers and torpedo boat destroyers.

Once the rendezvous had been reached and the ships were under the protection of the escorting destroyers, danger of attack from German underseas boats was practically negligible.

It was a very hazardous undertaking for a submarine to attack a protected convoy. Even if the attacking boat evaded detection until after she had succeeded in sinking her victim, escape, once her presence was known, was almost impossible, owing to the plan of attack adopted by the destroyer escort and the extravagant use of depth charges. The destroyers always formed a cordon around their charges, keeping about half a mile to a mile distant from them.

The ideal range for a submarine is between one hundred yards and one thousand yards. Torpedoes run at a maximum speed of forty knots at that range, and at this comparatively short range a miss is most unlikely. But if a submarine wished to attack a convoy, with reasonable hope of success, she was forced to make her shot from under the bows of the protecting destroyers, with the inevitable result that she was sighted and attacked. Should the submarine attempt a long shot, the chances of a hit were considerably reduced, but danger to herself from the escorting destroyers was only lessened to a minor degree.

The moment the torpedo was sighted, or its presence made known when it exploded, the speedy destroyers turned like lightning and raced along the course which the torpedo had followed and dropped their terrible depth bombs along its entire length. A line of air bubbles marked the course of the torpedo. When they reached the spot where they judged the submarine to be, they steamed in narrowing circles and dropped their bombs.

I don't say the submarine was always destroyed, but I can say that a crew which had once properly experienced an organized depth-charge attack and escaped usually picked next time victims less efficiently protected.

These circumstances drove the enemy submarines farther afield. They lurked in waiting on the trade routes followed by ships arriving from the south and the west as they approached their rendezvous.

We had British submarines patrol these positions. During the day the enemy submarines would rise to the surface and lie for hours scanning the horizon, looking for the wisp of smoke which announced the approach of a possible victim. The British submarines would patrol submerged all day, keeping a constant lookout through their periscopes for just such a beautiful pot shot.

The particular patrol I refer to took us well into the Bay of Biscay, where the shipping from the Mediterranean, South Africa, and South America all converged toward an area we had been given to protect and where the chances seemed favourable that we might encounter a Fritz. Moreover, we on *G-6* were all congratulating ourselves on getting away from the nerve-racking patrols we had recently been doing into the Bight of Heligoland.

We sailed November 29, 1917, and were hardly clear of harbour before a heavy rain began to fall, making it advisable to keep well clear of land. Heavy rain and fog at sea are bad enough in peace time, but during war time, when to sound one's fog horn is to invite attack from waiting submarines, it becomes a nightmare. Few can realize the strain one undergoes when in charge of the navigation and safety of a submarine under conditions of modern warfare. The speed of modern surface craft makes it impossible to use any form of challenge and reply unless you are on the surface during a bright day or a clear night. At all times it is the duty of those in a submarine to see without being seen. On the other hand, all surface patrol boats are instructed to sink on sight any submarine encountered, and waste no time in preliminaries.

The weather remained much the same till we reached our patrol position, then the wind gradually rose until it gained the velocity of a full gale. It was utterly impossible to attempt a submerged patrol in that kind of a sea, so we sank to a depth of about eighty feet and stayed under to escape the wave motion. It was found from experience that by descending to a depth which equalled about one and a half times the height in feet between the trough and crest of the waves on the surface, one could escape all wave motion.

Toward evening each day the air grew very stale, and we rose to the surface hoping the storm would have abated somewhat, but our hopes were doomed to disappointment. The gale raged more furiously than ever. We were forced to come up, however, for ventilation and to recharge our batteries, so we blew our tanks each evening, after bringing the boat head on to the mountainous seas.

These conditions prevailed for nearly two weeks and one evening as we broke surface a tremendous breaker—the kind that has made the Bay of Biscay famous—crashed against the superstructure, causing the boat to shudder and shake as if hit by a powerful ram. The shock caused several of the men who were standing in the control room to fall down.

The boat rolled and pitched like a crazy thing, until Coltart, the captain, opened the hatch and I followed him to the conning tower and connected the upper steering gear and brought her head to sea again.

The sea was an awe-inspiring sight. The waves were fully forty feet high and the roaring hurricane curled over their mighty crests, sending them rushing upon us like a milky Niagara. We both lashed ourselves to the periscope standard and waited to see how the boat would behave. I was steering and kept her riding at three quarters speed with the seas close to the starboard bow.

Considering the conditions, Submarine *G-6* behaved wonderfully. One moment we were rushing down the incline of one of the gigantic waves and the next a huge mountain of water, with curling white-topped crest, was threatening to overwhelm us. But the staunch little vessel rose gracefully over the oncoming breakers which expended their fury harmlessly under our keel.

As darkness closed down steering conditions became worse. It was more difficult to keep the boat's bow on to the sea. About midnight she was running on her Diesel engines and the batteries were charging satisfactorily. I was congratulating myself that in another hour or so we could again submerge into comparative comfort when a tremendous breaker seemed to fall short and tons of water crashed down on the conning tower. Sensing what was about to happen, I yelled below to the crew to shut off the engines and, waiting as long as I dared, shut down the hatch to prevent the waves swamping the boat.

To have left the hatch open would have been fatal, for the volume of water crashing down upon us would have flooded the control room and I knew that the torpedo ratings had some of the battery covers off for testing purposes. Had salt water leaked into the batteries, hydro-chlorine gas would have been generated and the interior of the boat made uninhabitable.

I had ordered the engines shut off because the oil engines consume air and can only be operated when the boat is on the surface. To have shut the hatch without shutting off the engines would have caused a vacuum in the boat, equally disastrous to those down below.

As the huge volume of water crashed down upon us the boat groaned and trembled with the shock of the blow. She seemed to pass right through the wave beneath the curling crest. The water strove to tear me from the lashings. I was submerged until my lungs seemed about to burst. Then the utter darkness grew less, we emerged, and I opened the hatch.

The submarine seemed to be standing right on her tail as if weighted down by the volume of water which had just passed over her. Suddenly, as the burden was released, she fell forward and crashed flat on her nose. The shock with which the outspread hydroplanes hit the surface is hard to describe, but it was such that the starboard hydroplane snapped off as one's fingers snap a carrot. The shock threw Holland-Pryor clean out of his bunk on to the deck.

As soon as circumstances permitted we dived and went below to quieter conditions. The loss of our starboard hydroplane was not our only damage. The engine-room artificer reported a badly cracked port propeller shaft, and investigation showed his report to be far from exaggerated. One flaw in the steel was almost one quarter inch wide. There we were minus the use of one hydroplane and one propeller, a lame duck seven hundred miles from home with a thousand fathoms of water under us.

Fortunately, the following day the gale blew itself out and the dangerous breakers gave place to huge rolling seas. When we were forced to the surface the next evening to recharge our batteries and to ventilate, *G-6* behaved admirably and we decided to return off patrol.

The other two officers and myself, who had shared the surface watches, were wet through and with no means of drying our clothes. The inside of the boat was cold and damp like an underground tunnel. The prolonged dives and resultant foul air, the nauseating smell of crude oil, the gassing of the batteries, and the terrible pitching and rolling of the boat had caused even the most experienced sailors among us to suffer from repeated vomiting spells.

Because the nearest dockyard where we could get necessary repairs done was Devonport, we headed for that port instead of returning to Bantry. We sent a wireless message informing the admiral commanding the port of our intentions, and notified him of the time of our probable arrival.

Proceeding on only one set of engines, we made poor time but finally rounded Cape Ushant and headed across the Channel where we were forced to dive several times to avoid convoys during the daytime. Controlling the boat while submerged on one motor and minus the starboard hydroplane was far from easy, especially when near the surface.

On the morning of the 18th of December we were proceeding on the surface and hoped to make port that evening in time for dinner. About 9 A. M. we sighted a convoy to the westward and dived. The convoy passed right over us and we distinctly heard the throb of the propellers. I was on watch and I waited fully ten minutes from the time the sounds had died away and then gave the order to rise to thirty feet.

The sea was still choppy. As I raised the periscope and looked in the direction of the receding vessels we broke surface accidentally. The convoy was at least two miles away and it was unlikely that they had seen us, so I turned the periscope around to make sure that all was clear elsewhere. I was horrified to see a destroyer not more than five hundred yards away and a little on our port quarter.

The men at the hydroplanes got the boat under control and she was soon completely submerged. I hoped we had escaped detection, but I was soon disillusioned.

Watching through the periscope, I saw the destroyer—an American one—turn and head right for us. As I looked I saw the black smoke belch from her funnels as she increased speed, and a white puff centred with a streak of flame came from her forward guns. There was nothing we could do but wait. There was no time to come to the surface and fire the recognition signals. Our fate lay in the hands of the gods.

My mind naturally flew to the forthcoming depth-charge attack and I decided to remain as near the surface as possible because I knew that the depth charges were set to explode at between eighty and one hundred feet. My reason told me that we were safer near the surface than deeper down, because the explosion would be farther away and the pressure less.

In an unbelievably short time the destroyer passed over us, so close that we actually felt her keel scrape our jumping wires. She had tried to ram us and failed. But as she passed over the spot where we had disappeared she laid her infernal eggs.

B-O-O-M!

The concussion shook the boat to the core. The stern raised up and the bows went down at a sickening angle. We went into a terrific nose dive. Many lights went out. Some of the electric fuses in the switchboard blew out. My gaze centred on the depth gauge. 60-70-80-90-100 feet, the indicator hand quickly flew. 120-130-150-160-180-200 feet, and still we went downward.

"Blow the main tanks!" Coltart had taken charge and issued the order.

I saw the electric hydroplane control was out of action—but there was no need to issue orders; the coxswain who happened to be on duty was putting them into hand gear. The angle the boat was diving at was easily 45 degrees. The low-pressure depth indicator only registered to 200 feet. The deep gauge showed 300 feet. That was as far as it would register.

The coxswain, with great presence of mind, had now the hydroplane controls into hand gear. His mate, who had been thrown from his stool when the boat took her perpendicular dive, scrambled back to his station. They whirled the wheels hard to rise. The hull was creaking and groaning under the terrific outside pressure of the water. Then she started to rise.

"Check the main tanks!" Coltart ordered.

I felt the boat straighten herself under the influence of the horizontal rudders and the added buoyancy.

"Shut off the air!"

Could we prevent her breaking surface again? That was the question which flashed through my mind. If not we would be easy victim of the destroyer's guns.

B-o-om! B-o-om! Crash! went two more depth charges, but they were farther away and did no more than jar us.

"Steady her at eighty feet!" The coxswain and his assistant at the hydroplane adjusted the horizontal rudders to check the boat from rushing to the surface. Still she rose, and water was ordered into Number 2 and Number 3 tanks. We arrested her upward rush at forty feet, and after a little juggling got complete control at sixty feet.

All I have recounted happened in less than two minutes and a great deal of credit must go to the men who had charge of the motors. Notwithstanding the fact that the explosion of the depth charge blew in the packing of the port shaft and allowed salt water to reach the motor which went off with a flash of blue flame and smoke that filled the after compartments, they stuck to their posts calmly and continued to work the starboard motor as instructed from the control room. It was fortunate that the explosion affected only the port motor, which was already useless owing to the cracked shaft. Otherwise this story would never have been told.

After anxiously waiting for upward of half an hour to see if the destroyer intended to renew its attack, we rose as cautiously as possible to the surface and took a look-see. The destroyer was evidently quite satisfied that she had done a good job, because she was hull down, headed straight for Plymouth.

Since all was clear, we came to the surface, hoisted our mast and flag—also our wireless to show we were innocent of any wrongful intentions —and headed after her. But all the world was against us that day. Although we had our flag flying and masts up, a fool of a trawler took a couple of shots at us before we could convince her that we were giving her the right challenge for the day. When she was convinced she kindly turned and escorted us into port.

After we were securely moored we made arrangements for the comfort of our crew and then Coltart, Pryor, and I headed for the officers' quarters at Devonport Barracks. Coated with brine and black with oil fumes, we looked like three stokers, but there was one thing we needed more than anything else, and that was a good stiff whisky and soda, so we entered the smoke room just as we were to order the drinks.

The room was crowded with officers waiting for dinner to be announced and in the centre of an in-

terested group were three American officers telling
of their good fortune in sinking an enemy submarine that morning.

"There was no question about it," the commander was saying. "She broke surface right under
our bows. We fired a couple of shots that seemed to
strike home; then we rammed her and, to make
sure, dropped three depth charges right over the
spot where she disappeared."

Coltart edged his way into the group.

"Sorry to disillusion you, old chap," he drawled,
"but it was my boat you tried to scupper. If a
whisky and soda or a cocktail will make up for the
D. S. O. you won't get, you are welcome to have
one on me, and here's wishing you better luck next
time."

Other submarines had equally narrow escapes
and others, less fortunate, were lost with most of
their crews. Owing to the almost instantaneous
nature of the action between submarines and surface ships, there was only one way in which our
anti-patrol boats could be given a clean break over
the enemy U-boats, and that was by permitting
them to attack without challenge any and every
submarine they sighted. Had they been forced to
hold their fire until they challenged the submarines
they sighted, they would never have sunk nearly
so many as they did. Fritz would have dived the
moment he saw the challenge. The arrangement

between our submarines and surface ships was simply, we were to see without being seen.

In February, 1918, *D-7,* in command of Lieu‧ tenant Tweedy, was patrolling in home waters when he sighted H. M. S. *Pelican* through the periscope. True to her name, she hesitated not at all about the kind of fish off which she would make her meal. She sighted the tip of *D-7's* periscope just as *D-7* sighted her. When she turned to ram the submarine the D-boat dived and altered course eight points, for she had no doubts about what would happen next.

Failing to find his quarry with his ram, the destroyer captain let go some depth charges. British submarines had contempt for those the enemy used; we had a great respect, however, for those carried by our own vessels. The *Pelican* dropped three depth charges. The explosions shattered several lights and smashed the after periscope. They also forced *D-7* to the surface. Quick action on the part of the submarine crew had the recognition signals working in a matter of seconds and the *Pelican* recognized them and was forced to deny herself further pleasure with the strange fish. The inquiry into this incident brought much cynical merriment to the Trade.

The anti-submarine experts found a great deal to interest them. They were happy beyond words to have an authentic record as to how their depth charges felt and worked, and they pointed out to those using them that a more accurate judging of speeds and distance would have allowed those on the *Pelican* to reduce materially the distance of one hundred and fifty yards (the estimated distance the charges were supposed to have exploded away from the submarine), and much better results could have been obtained.

Only a few days after *D*-7 had her experience, *L-2*, in charge of Lieutenant Commander Ackworth, had a run in with the American destroyers *Paulding, Davis,* and *Trippe*. The American destroyers sighted the conning tower of *L-2* as she accidentally broke surface for a moment.

Telling of the meeting, Ackworth said: "I lowered the periscope and dived to ninety feet. Just as I went down I heard the explosion of shells over me. I went down deeper to two hundred feet, and the first depth charge exploded, causing the after hydroplanes to jam hard-up. We went down at a steep angle by the stern and hit bottom at three hundred feet."

Four more heavy explosions were heard and flashes were seen in the boat. She was resting on the bottom with the bows up at an angle of 50 degrees. The sensation experienced when one is inside a submarine which assumes an almost perpendicular position is almost indescribable. I have heard a man tell about getting so tight that the pavement seemed to jump up and hit him in the face every time he took a step forward. I imagine that comes about as near as possible to describing what I felt like when we had our experience in *G-6*. I once had a similar experience when I tried to scramble out of a daycoach of a passenger train which had left the rails and fallen over the embankment to come to rest on its side.

"As the forward hydroplanes would not correct her trim," Ackworth continued, "I blew Number 5 and Number 6 tanks and she started to rise, but she did so at a tremendous angle. We broke surface, and as we did so the three destroyers opened fire on us at a range of about one thousand yards. One shot hit the pressure hull just abaft the conning tower. We fired the recognition signals and waved the white ensign at them. Firing ceased."

When it was all over one of *L-2's* crew remarked with reasonable bitterness: "Tripe is a blinkin' good name for them."

The anti-submarine authorities passed the following reassuring comment: "In view of the small amount of conning tower exposed and the distance at which it was sighted, the vessels are to be congratulated on the remarkable efficiency of their attack," or words with that general soothing effect.

I never heard just which of the G-boats it was, but one was sunk by our own destroyers. In the first place, the G-boat mistook her for an enemy ship and torpedoed her. The torpedo, however, failed to explode and the destroyer turned and rammed the luckless submarine. All her crew were lost with

the exception of one stoker. According to all the
rules of the game, he should have been the last
person to be saved. He was on duty in the engine
room when the bow of the attacking ship plowed
through the side of the compartment he was in,
practically cutting the boat in two. The boat filled
and sank immediately but he was carried to the surface in a huge bubble of escaping air and was
picked up by the crew of the attacking ship.

One of our H-boats, of which Lieutenant Lowther, R. N. R., with whom I served in *R-12,* was
the navigating officer at the time, torpedoed and
sank an Italian submarine which was encountered
on a patrol in the Adriatic.

Some of our boats had been sent out to help the
Italians. On this particular occasion the British
and Italian boats had gone out on patrol together.
They were given their respective areas to patrol
and in some way the Italian submarine got out of
her own patrol area and into that allocated to the
H-boat. Lowther sighted her just at daybreak and
dived. He attacked and closed to within one thousand yards. The torpedo exploded and blew into
the water a number of her crew who could be seen
standing on deck. When the British submarine rose
to the surface to rescue the survivors she found
they were Italians.

CHAPTER THIRTEEN

T HE extent and effectiveness of German submarine operations made necessary, early in the war,
a redistribution of our own forces. Before Q-boats
were thought of, and before the deadly depth
charge was invented, the commander in chief of
the Grand Fleet reorganized the whole submarine
fleet, with the purpose of operating principally
against the enemy U-boats. It was planned to patrol certain areas off the German coast, in the entrance to the Baltic, off the Norwegian coast, between the Orkney and Shetland islands, and off the
coast of Ireland, in the Bay of Biscay and English
Channel.

To facilitate the operation of these patrols, submarine bases were established all around the Brit-

ish Isles. In addition to the bases at Harwich and Blyth, there were others situated at Gorleston near Yarmouth, at Southbank on the Tees, at Rosyth, Scapa Flow, Killybegs on the northwest coast of Ireland, at Bantry Bay on the southwest coast, etc. In addition to these larger bases, from each of which twelve or more submarines operated, there were other bases from which the smaller and older types operated.

The patrols were placed in the most likely places to intercept inward- and outward-bound enemy submarines. They were set to ambush those of the enemy submarines which did succeed in escaping the vigilance of our patrols and get into lanes of shipping; they were also organized so that our submarines were in a position to keep track of the activities of enemy ships in or about Heligoland. The submarines patrolling in and around the Bight of Heligoland, off Terschelling, in the entrance to the Baltic and off the Belgian coast were based south of the Firth of Forth. Those in the Firth of Forth operated with the battle cruisers. Those based on Scapa Flow patrolled positions off the Norwegian coast and along the route it was known the enemy submarines travelled to reach the Atlantic. Those stationed off the Norwegian coast watched for U-boats which made for neutral waters, and then sailed for home, keeping well within the three-mile limit.

Those submarines based on the coast of Ireland

patrolled areas through which merchant ships and
transports passed when making for the positions
where the convoys formed to take them into British and French ports.

When not actually on patrol, the boats were on
stand-by duty, except for the period of the first
three days after they returned from patrol. They
were allowed this amount of time to give half their
crew leave and to get the boat reconditioned again
for service.

As eyes to the fleet, they had only one drawback.
The wireless equipment of those boats, commis-
sioned in 1914–15, was quite inadequate for the
purpose intended. This was rectified after a time
and the newer boats were fitted with sets powerful
enough to send in messages from any position on
patrol.

In addition to the normal adventures of their
kind, other strange tasks fell to the lot of the submarine patrols. If the destroyers were the police of
the sea routes about the British Isles, the submarines were the plain-clothes men, making their
presence known only when occasion demanded.
Such an occasion came after a spirited scrap between British and enemy destroyers on October
17, 1914, in which four of the enemy ships were
sunk off Texel. It was expected that the enemy
would retaliate, and about dawn our submarines
off Terschelling sighted the German ship *Ophelia.*
They kept her under observation and formed the

conclusion that she was nothing more nor less than a scout, although she pretended to be a hospital ship searching for possible survivors of the recent action. They never lost touch with her until Commodore Tyrwhitt came along with his flotilla and took charge of her. He ordered his men to dismantle her wireless and take her into a British port. The Naval Prize Court condemned the ship as a lawful prize, May 21, 1915, proving that the suspicions of the patrolling submarines were correct.

On another occasion our submarines were warned to watch for the German ship *Aud*. It was known she would leave Germany on a certain date with the renegade Irish knight, Roger Casement, on board. True to the information received, the *Aud* was picked up by our submarines one morning in April, 1916, and from that moment she was never lost touch with until she was picked up by our surface-patrol vessels. She was ordered to surrender off the west coast of Ireland after Sir Roger had been transferred to an enemy submarine which landed him on the Irish coast where he was arrested. Had it not been for our intelligence service and the coöperation of the submarines and surface ships in bringing about the undoing of that arch conspirator, it is hard to estimate what proportions the revolution which broke out in Ireland in Easter week, 1916, might not have reached.

No patrols done in or around the Bight of Heligoland were without some kind of excitement. I did about eight trips into those waters, and on each occasion we ran into something or other which kept our interest aroused. Sometimes it was aircraft which made matters uncomfortable, at other times it was speedy patrol vessels charging down on us at night, and rarely a trip passed without our getting in contact with an enemy submarine.

One morning I climbed up the conning-tower ladder to take a sight. I had previously looked around through the periscope to make sure all was clear, and it was. By the time we had blown our tanks and I had climbed the ladder and opened the hatch, an enemy submarine had done exactly the same thing about one hundred yards away. I was just lifting the sextant to my eye when I saw the U-boat. The officer on her conning tower saw me at exactly the same time. I don't know which of us was the most surprised. I know I dropped my sextant and it cost me thirty-five shillings to get it fixed.

In emergencies like that we had to think and act quickly. I yelled down the hatch: "Flood your starboard beam tube. Dive!" Then I jumped below, pulled the hatch down, and told Coltart that a U-boat was close to us on our starboard beam.

I remember now how I felt as I scrambled down the conning-tower ladder. I was sure she had seen us as soon as we broke surface. I hadn't seen the Fritz until I put the sextant to my eye, and then only when I was trying to make the sun cut the arc of the horizon. The glare of the sun was very bright and it took me some time to figure just what prevented my getting an even horizon. When I adjusted the coloured shades I saw the U-boat sitting there. As I climbed down the ladder, with every step I took I expected a shell to crash through the conning tower. But it was evident that the U-boat had got as big a surprise as I had. When we looked for her through the periscope she had gone.

Aircraft often attacked our submarines, but without doing them very much damage. We treated them with more or less contempt. We learned that their bombs were not very effective. The experience *E-31* had while on patrol off the enemy coast will probably remain unique in naval history, for she actually shot down and destroyed the zeppelin *L-7,* May 4, 1916. Our submarines were coöperating with the fleet. Two mine layers, the *Abriel* and the *Princess Margaret,* laid two mine fields, one to the south of Vyl Light and the other northwest of the Frisian Islands. The bait with which we hoped to coax the enemy to sea that day were the two seaplane carriers, the *Vendex* and the *Engadine.*

Their planes took the air soon after they arrived in position and flew inland, intending to drop their bombs on the zeppelin hangars at Londern. The plan was a good one. It was expected the enemy would come out and attack the two seaplane carriers, in which case the ships were ordered to run away and lead the enemy squadron to the position

where our submarines were waiting for them. Our
fleet was ready to close in behind them and force
them into the mine field. As usual, the plan didn't
work. Flying conditions were bad, only one plane
reached its objective, the enemy ships stayed in
harbour, and all they did was to send out zeppelins
to scout and report what all the fuss was about.

When *E-31* rose to the surface to ventilate, her
captain, Lieutenant Commander F. E. B. Fiel-
man, opened the hatch and saw a huge zeppelin
right above him. He wasted no time, gave the
alarm, and closed the hatch again. When the expected shower of bombs did not materialize, *E-31*
rose to periscope depth and took a look around.

The zeppelin was still there but much lower
than when first seen. A closer examination showed
that she was damaged and was trying to "lame-
duck it" back home. The officers of *E-31* realized
that the zeppelin must have undoubtedly notified
her own forces of her predicament, but decided
she was worth taking a chance for. They rose to the
surface and manned their gun.

The crippled airship hung as if suspended by an
invisible wire. She was settling lower and lower
but very slowly. When she was at an altitude of
not much more than three hundred feet the submarine's crew opened fire. Their guns bore at extreme
elevation. The airship looked big as a mountain.
The gunnery was like shooting at a barn door with
a shotgun. About ten rounds were all that were re-

quired to finish her. As the shells exploded, the hull burst into flames.

The crew of the burning ship climbed about like monkeys, trying to escape the flames and the heat. She sank lower and lower, hit the water and crumpled up. The crew of *E-31* took seven of the crew aboard, all they could accommodate. Enemy patrol boats and some seaplanes hove in sight, so *E-31* dived again and continued her patrol. She left the German ships to rescue the others who were still clinging to the wreckage of the zeppelin.

E-3, while patrolling off the mouth of the Ems in the early days of the war, also turned the tables on an enemy seaplane. Seeing the plane alight on the water, she rose to the surface and forced the pilot and mechanic to surrender. But *E-3* was too fond of hunting right in the enemy's own back yard. While doing the western Ems patrol in October, 1914, she went so close in shore looking for something to sink that she got cut off in a bay where the water was too shallow to allow her to escape. The enemy boats closed in on her. She was trapped. The sharp bows of the destroyers forced her to the surface and a few well-directed shells sent her to the bottom again, to stay.

(2)

In July, 1918, when I returned to submarines after being discharged from hospital, I went down to Harwich for a few days before I was appointed

navigator to Submarine *K-12*. While there, I saw
at first hand the results of one of the worst tragedies
of the war. A squadron of enemy seaplanes returning from a daylight raid on Lowestoft and Walmer
caught *C-25* napping. The boat was a bloody
shambles when she arrived back in port, with her
captain and seven of her crew dead.

C-25 was patrolling on the surface, off the south-
east coast. She was not very far from land when
the crew saw the planes coming from the westward. They gave little heed to them, thinking they
were a squadron of British planes heading for the
coast of Flanders. The planes also sighted the submarine but completely ignored her and kept on going until they got into the sun, then they turned
and swooped down on their unsuspecting victim.

There were five seaplanes in the flight, and they
all opened up on the C-boat at point-blank range.
Although taken completely by surprise, the crew
of the submarine got their Lewis gun on deck,
intending to fight back. The seaplanes concentrated a withering fire on the conning tower and
the captain and three men slumped to the deck,
dead or wounded before they could fire the first
round. Conditions were equally bad inside the
boat. Compared to the hulls of modern submarines,
her hull was nothing more than a sardine can. The
hull was pierced in several places and more men
killed. The bullets seemed to go through the thin
plating as easily as through cheese.

But it is conditions such as these that provide the medium of illustrating the finest traits in man. The captain was dead on the conning tower; the mere youth who was first lieutenant of the boat took command. He climbed up the conning-tower ladder to investigate and was told by Leading Seaman Barge, who was the only man alive above, "Dive, sir. Don't worry about me. I'm done for anyway." His only concern was for the safety of his boat and the rest of her crew. If she dived before the seaplanes made a sieve out of her, she might escape and get back to port.

Down below, men were plugging the bullet holes as they appeared in the hull. The young lieutenant, ignoring his leading seaman's appeal, struggled to get him below. He succeeded, but only those who know what the conning tower of a C-class submarine is like can realize what a task he had . . . and Barge died as he was deposited on the floor of the control room.

Just as they were about to dive one of the bodies fell from above and prevented those below closing the lower hatch. A leg protruded through the hatch and hung down into the control room so that it was impossible for anyone to climb into the confined space in the conning tower. The crew struggled to move the body—but it was jammed into an almost immovable position. If the leg hadn't been sticking down they might have managed to shut the hatch. Bullets hummed through the conning tower like bees through a hive.

Either the hatch had to be closed or the boat was lost. With the lad in command, to think was to act. He ordered the men to get him a knife and a saw; he dismembered the limb and closed the hatch. Meantime, the crew, with commendable coolness, were plugging the bullet holes as fast as they appeared in the hull. Two men were killed while doing this duty. Just as they were ready to dive they discovered their motors had been put out of commission. Escape seemed hopeless. Then they heard the sound of heavy gunfire. The bullets stopped coming through.

They opened the hatch again. The seaplanes had been caught napping. An E-class submarine returning from patrol had opened fire on them and they were driven off and *C-25* was towed into port. When she arrived alongside the depot ship, the interior of the boat looked like nothing so much as a slaughter house. Blood was spattered everywhere. The dead and wounded were taken from the boat as tenderly as possible and rushed to hospital.

(3)

Strange things used to happen around the various lightships which the submarines of both nations used as a means of fixing their position. The *Ship-*

wash, the *Sunk,* the *Hinder* and the *Mass* were all used a great deal; our boats, patrolling off the enemy coast, would use the *Hinder* lightvessel to fix their positions before going into the narrow channels and shallow waters to do their patrols, and the enemy mine-laying submarines would use British lightships to fix their position before proceeding to lay their mines in the entrance to our harbours. Naturally all boats used to fight shy of remaining on the surface in these locations by day, but at night it was no uncommon occurrence for several boats to be on the surface at the same time, charging their batteries.

The officers on the British submarines would know that only one other boat was supposed to be in that same position and would be worried to find themselves in company with three and sometimes even four submarines at the same time. It was a problem to know in the darkness which was friend and which was foe. We had, of course, a challenge we could have used, but if the other boat failed to recognize it, the crew would fire the instant the challenge was made, often with disastrous results.

Lieutenant A. C. Bennett, in command of *C-19,* had two such experiences. On the night of March 1, 1917, he was on the surface in the vicinity of the *Hinder* lightship when he sighted, in the moonlight, another very small submarine steering right for him. He knew other British submarines were supposed to be in the vicinity and was, therefore,

rather in a quandary to know whether it was an
enemy boat or one of our own. Gazing through his
night glasses, he thought she was another C-boat
and challenged her. The other boat did the same
thing. Each failed to recognize the other's signal.
C-19 unfortunately had no gun. She therefore
manœuvred so as to bring her bow tubes to bear.
While doing so the other boat flashed the ordinary
Morse signal IMI, meaning "Repeat." Both had
drifted to within one hundred yards of each other
by this time and to his astonishment the commander of *C-19* heard himself hailed by the other
boat in German.

Just as he was about to fire the tubes, the enemy
vessel put her helm hard over and headed away
from *C-19*. A merry chase started and *C-19* was
gaining when the U-boat fired a star shell. *C-19*
fired back with rifles and revolvers. Bennett could
do nothing more effective. Only the larger and
newer boats had been fitted out with guns.

Consternation reigned on the conning tower of
the U-boat. Some person called out as if seeking
aid from below and then the boat did a splendid
crash dive just in time to escape a torpedo *C-19*
fired at her. I heard afterward that news was received from Germany that the shots fired by *C-19*
had taken effect and killed the captain of the
U-boat.

Evidently the U-boat dived at such an angle
and speed that she hit bottom and bounced back

up to the surface again, and those on the conning
tower of the C-boat saw the periscope appear mo-
mentarily as her crew struggled to get the boat
trimmed and under control. As the tip of the periscope showed in the moonlight, Bennett put his
helm over and tried to ram the German boat, but
he passed over it without striking anything solid.

It has always been a trait of British born officers
to use the ram during times of war. Our American
cousins used often to refer to this and say, "You
fellows seem to be able to ram anything and get
away with it."

This was true. There was something extraordi-
narily fascinating in rushing a ship worth millions
at another ship, to sink one and probably both of
them, to get congratulations and possibly decorations for doing something that in ordinary circumstances would call for a court-martial or a
naval court of inquiry.

I know of dozens of cases where the officer of
the watch tried to ram other vessels sighted during
the night I never knew of a case where one tried to
avoid ramming an enemy vessel or neglected to
seize an opportunity when it offered. We considered it the surest and most effective method of attack.

On March 5th Lieutenant Bennett met another
enemy submarine. It was blowing a living gale.
March had opened like a "roaring lion" and the
sea was kicking up such a shindy that no torpedo

could be expected to run with any degree of accuracy.

Feeling quite safe under the circumstances, an enemy vessel rode into the seas taking little notice of *C-19,* for the German U-boat officers never seemed to have any inclination to try and ram one of our boats, perhaps because the type of pistol they used in the war heads of their torpedoes was far more easily touched off than ours.

Bennett steered so as to get as close as possible to the enemy vessel and, asking the engine-room ratings for every bit of speed possible, turned and steered right for the U-boat. He instructed the men he had waiting on the conning tower to fire with their rifles at the men on the enemy's conning tower, hoping they might hit some of them and delay the boat's diving. I don't know if any were hit or not, but the U-boat dived and all *C-19* hit was the periscope, smashing it off.

An official report reads: "Lieutenant A. W. Forbes, in *C-7* sighted a large U-boat on his port quarter at 3:32 A. M. It was dark and misty at the time. He immediately attacked on the surface, and sank her with a single shot at 250 yards' range." That is the cold plain statement which officially records the deed. Having had similar experiences which did not, however, terminate so successfully, I will try to explain what performing that deed was like.

Picture a dismal night in the month of April. A

dank Scotch mist hanging over everything, the sea like a lake of ink, the heavens seeming to hang so low that you feel you can reach up and touch them. A night dark and weird—dark as the inside of a cow, as one signal rating I served with once remarked. It is the hour between midnight and 4 A. M., known to all sailors as the graveyard watch —the time when life seems at its lowest ebb, when most ailing people release their hold on life, and slip out into the unknown.

The boat would be lying there on the surface like a sleeping whale. Suddenly the officer on watch would sight the other submarine hardly discernible against the neutral background of the night. Doubt would immediately assail him. Was she friend or was she foe? Perhaps other British boats were expected to rendezvous there, and to wait for the dawn and the sweepers which would clear a way for them into the harbour. This was a necessary procedure, for the enemy submarines mined the channels leading to our bases, just as we mined theirs.

The officer on watch would call the captain and together they would study the low, dark form through the night glasses. They dared not challenge, for if she were an enemy boat she would attempt to sink them or dive the moment she saw the signal.

They would continue to stare through the glasses until their eyes were strained and imagination ran riot. Then they would perhaps order the motors

ahead ever so slowly, so as to drift closer to the
other vessel.

Every nerve would be strained. They would be
praying for light and the night would seem to
grow darker. The blackness of the night would
seem to weigh down on them like a heavy wet blanket, clammy and cold. A cloud of heavy mist would
drift by and for a moment they would lose sight of
the other vessel altogether. Then she would appear
again like a ghost emerging from beneath the
shroud of fog which had enveloped her. Again eyes
would strain through the inverted lenses of the
night glasses. Then the moment of decision would
come. Both would agree the other vessel was a
Fritz. They would point out her peculiarities to
each other. The boat would be manœuvred to bring
the tubes to bear. They would wait in suspense until the bows stopped swinging, wondering if the
other boat was aware of their presence. Then the
captain would give the command F-I-R-E!

A startled cry might float across the comparatively small distance which separated the boats as
the lookouts on the enemy's conning tower sighted
the phosphorescent trail of the deadly tin fish racing toward them. Then would come the dull heavy
B-O-O-M, a blinding flash would rend the night, the
torpedoes in the enemy boat would explode to add
further chaos, to be followed by a moment of
deathlike silence until the débris began to fall
splashing into the water all around.

Such was the actual experience of Lieutenant P. Phillips when in command of *E-52*. He sent *UC-63* to her doom and there was one survivor only. That was a petty officer. He gave the German version of what happened: "The night being cold, the navigating officer sent the A. B., who was on watch with him, below to get some coffee. In the meantime the engineer of the boat came on the bridge and stood talking to the officer of the watch, who in consequence failed to keep a proper lookout. Chancing to look to port, I suddenly saw a submarine on the surface. We put the helm over and were just starting to turn when the torpedo struck amidships."

That was all. It is enough, however, to show that victory goes to the alert. The conning tower of a submarine is no place in which to gossip or doze. The attention of the officer of the watch on the conning tower of *UC-63* had probably not been distracted for more than a few seconds, but it was long enough to cause death to all but one of her crew.

(4)

Once when returning from patrol in *G-6* we attacked a Fritz but missed her and she dived. For more than an hour we hunted her with the use of our hydrophones, intending to ram her. We had a most exciting hour dodging around in an effort to get the sounds of the enemy's propeller to register right ahead. When they did, we would charge full speed in the direction we believed Fritz to be. Our luck was either in or out, according to the point of view.

E-50 did a real piece of work, or, to use the vernacular of the Trade, a real job of work. She managed to ram a Fritz under water. To me the story is one of the greatest of underseas warfare. I heard the details in the ward room of one of the depot ships shortly after it happened.

E-50 was on patrol when one of the crew heard what he thought were sounds of another submarine's motors. Just then the officer keeping the periscope watch sighted the periscope of another submarine. One quick glance and he recognized it as of different appearance to those our boats used. Taking the periscope tip as his mark, he fired the forward torpedoes but failed to make a hit. He charged the other boat and a collision followed.

His actions had been governed simply by the motto "Get your enemy!"

What followed was like the fight to a finish between two amphibian monsters. The stem of the E-boat had bitten into the hull of the U-boat and remained embedded in her back. The hydroplanes of the British boat jammed tight. What could they do next? The ocean bed was two hundred feet below them. The pressure was great. Would the strained plates of the submarine withstand that terrible outside pressure or would the sides cave in? The men stood silently watching their commanding officer and wondering what he intended to do. The action of the enemy made up his mind for him. In a silence like that of a tomb the crew of the E-boat could hear the sounds made by the crew of the other boat. They heard them frantically blowing their tanks. They were trying to get to the surface.

"Must be damaged more than we are," was the laconic remark of the British commander to those standing around him. "He must be leaking. He seems damned anxious to get topside. . . . Flood all our tanks. We'll keep him down."

His orders in such a situation are almost unbelievable but the most extraordinary thing is that his men obeyed his orders without hesitation and the tanks were flooded. As the other boat frantically blew and pumped the water out of her tanks and flooded compartment, the E-boat filled hers to counteract the other's buoyancy. They held the U-boat under until all sounds died—died as the men must have died inside her—and the two boats went swirling crazily downward toward the ocean floor.

Suddenly those in the British boat felt the enemy vessel break loose. They felt her drag along her side, bumping as she drifted astern.

E-50, with jammed hydroplanes and heavy with negative buoyance, started down for the ocean bed alone. For four anxious minutes her crew struggled to make her rise. Suddenly she shot to the surface as the water was forced out of her tanks. She saw the conning tower of her adversary on her quarter. It was listed over to starboard. The German submarine seemed to be heavily down by the bows and sinking fast. *E-50* searched around but nothing more was seen but a rapidly increasing area covered with oil bubbling up out of the depths below like the life blood from a harpooned whale.

No episode of the air could be so terrible. It might be more spectacular because others could watch such a duel from the earth, but it could not reach the same limits of horror for it could not last so long. If two planes ram each other they must crash to earth in a few seconds. The death agony in a submarine is longer. The men in that German boat had to watch death creep upon them through the damaged hull. They would gasp and choke as the deadly chlorine gas was generated as the salt water reached the batteries. They had no back door . . . no escape. They could not jump and trust to a parachute.

CHAPTER FOURTEEN

ALL the world knows that the enemy U-boats very nearly brought Britain to her knees. It became imperative that they be destroyed in such numbers that the German shipbuilding yards could not keep pace with the losses. The more enemy submarines we sank, the fewer trained crews there were left to man the new boats. It was also seen that if our anti-submarine patrols could be so organized that they were able to sink enemy submarines in great numbers, the morale of those crews which escaped might break. This did, in fact, happen toward the end of the war. Germany had very few U-boats at sea for two months before the armistice was signed. And the life of a U-boat was considered less than three months.

It so happened that while I was serving in *G-6* we received orders to leave Blyth and proceed around the entire British Isles, relieving other boats which were due for refit, or temporarily replacing others which had been lost in the execution of their duty. This gave me a wonderful opportunity to learn what was going on at other depots. I took *G-6* to Scapa Flow, to Bantry Bay, to Harwich, and to Southbank on the Tees.

Because of the fact that the English Channel had been completely blocked against submarines at the eastern end across the Strait of Dover, the enemy U-boats had to go around the north coast of Scotland to reach the Atlantic and merchant shipping approaching or leaving British ports.

To save time, they were using the Fair Island Channel which separates the Orkney from the Shetland Island group. We learned that the procedure was for enemy submarines to leave Germany by way of the Baltic, keep close to the coast of Norway until they reached about latitude 50 degrees north, and then strike across for Fair Island. We sent our submarines to patrol where it seemed most likely they would find enemy submarines on the surface charging their batteries or fixing their positions. Our wireless direction finders were often able to fix the position of an enemy submarine when she used her wireless several times during the night and thus enable the officers of British submarines to plot the enemy vessel's course and speed. Having obtained this information, we would proceed at full speed, head the enemy off, submerge, and wait for her to show up. The British submarines which patrolled these northern waters also kept a sharp lookout for mine layers and disguised raiders seeking to run the blockade of the 10th Cruiser Squadron. Enemy submarines were anxious to sneak through Fair Island channel submerged during the middle of the day so as to be well clear of land and free from our patrols before they came to the surface again at night to charge their batteries. They either had to do that or take a chance on running through on the surface at night and risking attack from the numerous trawlers and other craft which patrolled in that vicinity.

It is my own personal opinion we lost some of the boats engaged in this work because they stayed too much on the surface during the hours of daylight. It was very tempting to come to the surface about 10 A. M. and again at noon to obtain sights and ventilate the boat, especially during the summer months. The days in those northern latitudes were long. The heat caused the batteries to gas. The air inside the boats became so foul you could taste it. It was, however, a dangerous practice.

E-22 was sunk April 25, 1916, by *UB-18, E-49* was lost off the Shetland Islands, March, 1917. We lost *C-34* July 21, 1917. She was on the surface and was sunk by the enemy submarine *U-52*.

But extraordinary bad luck was suffered by the

G-class submarines. While not one of the G-class from *G-1* to *G-6* was lost, although engaged in overseas patrols where mines and enemy patrols were thickest, the higher-numbered boats had the worst possible run of luck, starting with the loss of *G-9* in September, 1917. In numerical order, *G-8* went in January, 1918. *G-7* was the next to go, but when we in *G-6* began to think that our time on earth was running pretty short, the whim of Fate changed and the next boat to meet disaster was *G-11*.

I remember the loss of *G-8* only too well. Lieutenant Watson, R. N. R., her navigator, was the life of the whole depot when he was in port. We had christened him George Robey. He could impersonate the famous comedian in a way which provided us with hours of entertainment. We arrived in harbour after a terrible trip. *G-8* should have arrived from patrol about the same time. In fact she should have been in ahead of us. One of my brother officers went straight home on three days' leave, and when he returned he walked into the smoke room of the depot ship in ignorance of the fact that *G-8* was overdue. He sensed a sort of gloom as he entered the smoke room.

"What's the matter with you fellows to-night?" he demanded jokingly. "Where's Watson? Why isn't he at the piano? Hey! Watson, old chap, where are you?" he yelled, thinking he was possibly in the adjoining room playing cards. But Watson had sung his last song, and played his last game of cards.

But our boats didn't have all the bad luck. In fact our submarines actually sank eighteen of the enemy U-boats we caught napping, and we attacked and fired torpedoes at dozens of others that escaped.

The successful attack made by Lieutenant Varley, commanding officer of *H-5,* stands out above all others because of the circumstances under which it was performed.

I have said before that some boats and their crews never seemed to get an opportunity to test their skill against the enemy at all, while others seemed to make contact with the enemy every time they put to sea. Lieutenant Varley grew tired of doing monotonous patrols. He longed for action. He was very young, very quiet, and, incidentally, very fed-up. Not with the war, or submarines, or the rotten weather one usually experienced while on patrol, but with the enemy. He was fed-up because they wouldn't come out and give him the chance to put holes in their bottoms. He was sent to patrol a position in the Bight of Heligoland which he didn't consider "worth a damn." There was nothing doing. He got bored stiff. He felt reasonably certain that if the powers that be would only allow him to go on a hunt of his own he could stir up something. He had no false notions as to what the Noble Lords' answer would be if he asked them to allow him to go off on an independent cruise. So he didn't ask, he went.

He did a most terrible and unheard-of thing. He left his patrol position without permission and wandered off into the enemy's front garden. The youthful submarine officer reasoned that if he were successful the facts of his escapade were bound to leak out, but the success achieved would probably temper the wrath of their Lordships. If he were unsuccessful he could return to his original position and say nothing about the little jaunt he planned to take. If he got tangled in nets or mine fields and was killed, no explanations would be needed. So one fine day in July, 1916, he fixed his position by Terschelling Light and proceeded as requisite for the mouth of the Ems.

He arrived at his hunting grounds at 2 A. M. and dived off Borkum. He was where the enemy would least expect to find him. His patience and daring availed him nothing all that day. His brother officers and his crew were all keen for the adventure, so they decided to remain a while longer. They came to the surface after nightfall but were forced by enemy destroyers to dive about 10:30 P. M. They were back on the surface again within an hour and, avoiding patrol vessels, managed to charge their batteries. They then proceeded east, leaving the enemy's front garden, and went right into his vestibule. Before dawn they were submerged again off Wangeroog Light. Good hunting ground this, but nothing showed up to break the monotony of another day's patrol. Toward night they moved carefully through the narrow, shallow channels to a position where they would have a better chance to charge their batteries without interference and without giving their position away. They got into a position to the northwest of the *Aussen Jade* lightship. About 10 P. M. they sighted a destroyer. Two hours later, just as they were finishing their charge and all was ready for trouble, trouble came in the shape of a flotilla of enemy destroyers. The night was light and Varley attacked the flotilla, but without success. He and his crew were bitterly disappointed.

He was not only disappointed but was annoyed. Everything was going wrong. During the preceding day his periscope had become stiff to turn. Instead of turning with the jewel movement of a watch, it turned more like the old capstan on a sailing ship. While on the surface he and a couple of his men had tried to fix it. They were busy fixing it when the destroyers came along and tried to fix them. They were forced to make a crash dive and lose all their tools in the bargain. He wondered what he should say in his report to explain the loss. He was far from happy. Everything had gone wrong since he had left his proper patrol position. His thoughts were far from pleasant when the offi-

cer who relieved him at the periscope at 10 A. M.
reported sighting a Fritz.

Here was a chance. It was considered almost,
if not quite, as important to sink an enemy submarine as it was to sink a battleship. The submarine
certainly did more damage and was more of an influence on the possible outcome of the war than
any two battleships. They were always in port.

The sea was rather rough and the water in the
channel shallow. Depth keeping was difficult, and
to make matters worse it took two men besides himself to move the periscope. Notwithstanding all
these difficulties, he succeeded in his attack on the
U-boat. Just as she was about to enter her own harbour the torpedo exploded and blew her skyward.
Varley felt he must take some tangible proof back
with him. He felt it was absolutely necessary because now he would have to explain how he was
short one torpedo. He felt if he could only take one
prisoner home with him it might go a long way
toward appeasing the wrath of the Brass Hats
when he reported that he had left his patrol position. He rose to the surface headed for some men
swimming in the water. The destroyers and patrol
boats took serious objection to this final piece of
impudence. They opened fire on him and forced
him to dive again before he could smuggle one
Fritz aboard. They carried their animosity further. Owing to the shallowness of the water, they
kept him under all day and swept for him. Then

they gave him a lively session dropping depth charges all around him, but didn't seem to be able to register a direct hit.

In his report Varley remarked. "I did not consider it advisable to attack the searching destroyers because of the stiffness of my periscope." It is not recorded whether their Lordships accepted his apology or not. His report written upon his return to Harwich also stated: "We registered many explosions inside of *H-5* that day. One very heavy one. We also heard sweeping wires scrape the whole length of the boat."

When he finally extracted himself from the mess he took up his proper patrol position and then returned to Harwich and reported his success and his "slight transgression from orders."

He got merry hell from the captain in charge of the depot, who threatened him with a court-martial. But having given him a most terrible calling down himself, the captain shielded him as much as possible from the wrath of the Lords of the Admiralty. He wrote them to this effect: "Lieutenant Varley is a very able and gallant submarine officer, and although there is no possible excuse for his disregarding his orders and proceeding to patrol off the mouth of the Weser, it is submitted, however, that his skillful and successful attack on the enemy submarine may be taken into consideration, more particularly because of the fact that he was handicapped by a defective periscope. The fine conduct of Lieutenant Varley and his crew while being depth-charged might also be considered in mitigation of the offense."

None of the crew of *H-5* were hung, drawn, or quartered for their terrible breach of discipline, but it was more than a year before their Lordships condoned the breach by decorating Varley and his gallant crew for their gameness. Admiral S. S. Hull who commanded the entire British submarine forces personally interceded on Varley's behalf and obtained for him his D. S. O.

(2)

Lieutenant C. Barry, D. S. O., with whom I served in submarine *R-12* as his navigator, won his decoration for the manner in which he attacked and sank the enemy submarine *UB-72* in the early part of 1918. He was on patrol in the English Channel, keeping a sharp lookout for enemy submarines which were playing havoc with our merchant ships, when he received a wireless message about midnight one night telling him that an enemy submarine had been seen in a certain position at dusk the night before. It so happened that a convoy of troop ships was due to pass that very position a little after daybreak the following morning.

Was it possible that in some way Fritz knew the intentions of the approaching transports? Barry set off to investigate. He had to go full speed to make it and he charged his batteries as he raced toward the position indicated in the message.

He took no chances on running into the enemy submarine in the dark and dived as soon as he got into the position reported. Then came the anxious watching for the dawn. Would they sight the enemy submarine on the surface? Would she dive with the coming of day or would she remain on top scanning the horizon until she sighted the smoke of the approaching transports? You can see so much farther from the top of the conning tower that Barry reasoned that the chances were, she would stay on top until she actually sighted the troop ships.

Dawn broke and the ocean stretched around them with not a solitary thing in sight. The temptation was great to start and move about looking for the illusive submarine, but then the officers in the British submarine reasoned that if the enemy submarine was working from information it would surely wait in the position the convoy would be in about eight o'clock.

A ship usually gives her position as at the four-hour intervals. Charts and information with regard to the movements of expected convoys were taken from the safe and studied. The officers checked their position over carefully and then proceeded to the exact position the transports were due at 8 A. M.

They sighted Fritz sitting on the surface pretty

as a hen. There was really nothing to it after that. They closed to within six hundred yards and *UB-72* continued to roost there while her officers stood on the conning tower gazing through their binoculars in the direction from which the transports were expected.

She was stopped, but Barry intended to take no chances. He fired both bow tubes and both torpedoes hit, one forward the other aft. When the smoke cleared there was nothing to be seen. Barry ordered surface stations and headed over to the spot where the submarine had been. Three or four men were swimming about like dazed fish in the water.

Three survivors were saved, and after they were taken on board and given dry clothes and hot drinks one of them who could speak English wanted to know why the British crew had troubled to pick them up out of the water. He said that the crews of all German submarines had been informed that it was no use to surrender as the British hung all the survivors of U-boats as pirates after they got them ashore.

It is quite evident that those three were not hung, for about four months afterward we received a bill forwarded to *R-12* through the British Red Cross claiming a sum of about $12.50, "for goods stolen for souvenirs."

I don't think the bill was ever paid, and the man who had dived into the icy water to save one of the crew remarked, "If you pay that bill, sir, I'll never forgive myself—blowed if I will."

As I mentioned before, blind chance seemed to govern what happened in submarines. Barry and some of his crew were transferred to *R-12* and others replaced them. *D-6* fell victim to the well-aimed torpedo of an enemy submarine immediately after she resumed her patrols again.

Lieutenant Bradshaw, D. S. O., commanding officer of *G-13,* made what might be considered the luckiest shot of the war. He sank an enemy submarine when he fired at her at what was estimated as seven thousand yards range. It was generally believed that the boat he sank was the famous *Bremen,* sister ship to the *Deutschland* which journeyed across the Atlantic to New York.*

Bradshaw sighted the large submarine while doing a submerged patrol. He manœuvred and fired his two bow-torpedo tubes. He missed with both. He figured he had made a mistake in estimating the enemy's speed. He put his helm over and brought his starboard-beam tube to bear and, allowing a little more deflection, fired again. Once more there was no result. He manœuvred and brought his other beam tube to bear and with a prayer on his lips gave the order to fire again. He had wasted about eighteen thousand dollars' worth of torpedoes with his first three shots and he was more than anxious that the fourth should register

---

*I have since learned it was the *Bremen.*—W. G. C.

a hit. But the expected explosion never materialized.

Figuring he might as well be killed for a sheep as a lamb when he got back, he turned his stern to the fast-disappearing enemy U-boat and let go the twenty-one-inch torpedo. To the amazement of every one of the crew, they distinctly felt the explosion register in the boat at the proper interval after the torpedo had been fired. The Admiralty were inclined to doubt the report, and unkind enough to say that they in no way wished to insinuate that the crew had not felt an explosion register in the boat, but they thought it likely some mines had been exploded by sweepers, or something to that effect. However, Bradshaw, I believe, was finally credited with the wonderful shot, and decorated for it. He deserved it anyway. He was an exceptionally fine type of officer, and had sunk the enemy submarine *UC-43,* March 10, 1917, when patrolling off Muck le Flugga Light.

(3)

Commander Robert H. T. Raikes in *E-54* accounted for two German submarines. I served with him for a time when *G-6* was stationed at Bantry Bay. He bagged both his Fritzes within a period of four months. And how we other officers envied him! The first he sank with ridiculous ease. I don't know how true the story was as told to me, for some sailors are awful fellows to spin a yarn, but it is worth repeating. According to my informant, Raikes returned and reported that he had sunk an enemy submarine in position so-and-so and had rescued no less than seven survivors.

That was an unusually large number to be saved from a boat sunk by torpedo attack. Raikes, as I remember him, was a rather quiet sort of man, never spoke much, but had a certain dry humour and sarcastic wit. After dinner was over the officers were sitting around in the smoke room when one asked, "How on earth did you come to save seven of the blighters?'

"It was Sunday morning," Raikes replied, "and they appeared to be up on the surface sunning themselves and washing their clothes. Just as I was about to fire the torpedoes one man provided himself with a pail and proceeded to pay his tribute to Nature."

"What did you do then, sir?" asked a very youthful and inexperienced officer who performed the duties of assistant paymaster on the depot ship.

"Why, I saved him the trouble of using toilet paper. What would you expect me to do . . . hold his hand?"

The facts as I know them to be are that *E-54* left for patrol and before she had gone far from her base sighted no less than three U-boats, one after the other. She attacked them all and fired torpedoes at the first two without securing a hit. The last, Raikes blew all to pieces and brought in seven prisoners.

His other adventure was far more exciting. He was doing a patrol near certain neutral waters where enemy submarines were reported to gather. It was during the latter part of August and he was to remain on patrol seven days. All he saw the first four days was a neutral warship doing target practice. On the fifth day he sighted a U-boat. It was Raikes' luck to see them in bunches or he would have been out of luck, for he missed the first one after manœuvring nearly half an hour to get a shot at her.

He did a splendid attack and got to within six hundred yards, but by estimating the enemy's speed as eleven knots when it was more likely to have been six or seven, both shots missed ahead. Fritz saw the torpedoes flash past and dived in time to miss the third torpedo. Raikes was certainly a marvel at getting rid of torpedoes. He had thrown away about thirty thousand dollars' worth that day.

Within an hour and a half the same Fritz or another appeared on the surface. Raikes set off after her. He wanted to make up for all those torpedoes he had wasted. In attempting to head her off and get into a good position for a shot, *E-54* grounded on a sand bank. I was told that after Raikes had finished cursing his luck the air inside the boat was so charged with brimstone and sul-

phur that it was almost necessary to ventilate. They
managed to get the boat off without any serious
damage and within an hour sighted yet another
U-boat, or the same one. She was coming down the
same channel.

Raikes was determined to get Fritz this time but
once more he grounded while manœuvring to get
into position to fire. This time he was forced to
the surface and Fritz disappeared. She was about
a mile away at the time. But again that afternoon
he sighted his quarry or another one and that
U-boat also escaped without his getting a chance
to fire a torpedo. Could worse luck be imagined?

Next day luck changed, however, for he shifted
his position and went back to where he had seen
the neutral warship practising. About four bells
in the afternoon watch another Fritz was sighted.
He speeded up on the motors and chased her for
half an hour. He got into the most favourable of all
positions, about eight points on the enemy's bow.
He fired at her as she passed at four hundred
yards' range and one torpedo hit. There were no
survivors. This annoyed Raikes because he was
curious to know if he had been chasing the same
boat all the time or whether he had been in company with a regular fleet of commerce raiders.

Lieutenant D'Oyly Hughes, who had served
with Nasmith in the Dardanelles, had an extraordinary experience while in command of submarine
E-35. He torpedoed and sank a U-boat after

an attack which lasted two hours and a half. When
he came to the surface to rescue the survivors he
was nearly torpedoed himself by another Fritz.
He had to dive and leave the enemy to drown. The
strange thing about Hughes' experience was that
it is quite evident that the U-boat he torpedoed
was waiting to rendezvous with her consort, for
she patrolled up and down on the surface the whole
two and a half hours. Hughes had spotted her
through his periscope and manœuvred to head her
off. When he reached the position which would
have put him on the enemy's bow he raised his
periscope only to find she had altered course and
was off in another direction. He set off after his
quarry again only to have the same thing happen.
In this way he used up nearly all the juice in his
batteries. He had about given it up as a bad job
when the U-boat turned once more and came past
him on a course which just about made a miss impossible. Hughes took no chances, however. He
fired two torpedoes and both hit. The first made
little or no noise but threw up a lot of water and
débris. The second torpedo made a tremendous
noise and the concussion felt in *E-35* was severe
enough to put out some of the lights, although the
effect of the explosion did not seem to be nearly so
great as that of the first, which had made so much
less noise.

It seems that the other U-boat heard the explosion as well. As *E-35* rose from the depths and her

first lieutenant, coxswain, and an able seaman got ready to fish aboard three or four of the U-boat's crew who were seen clinging to some wreckage or a small raft, the other Fritz appeared. Hughes dived to attack at once, as was his duty, and it was lucky he did, for he had no sooner got under than the crew distinctly heard a torpedo pass them. A moment's delay and they would in all probability have joined their own victim on the floor of the ocean.

CHAPTER FIFTEEN

T HIS book would be incomplete if some mention was not made of the smaller incidents which so frequently enlivened the patrols of all those who served in the under-water branch of the service.

Time after time in the official reports made in connection with these incidents the commanding officer of the boat involved would write something like the following: "I find it impossible to say in words what would do justice to the conduct of my crew. It is equally impossible to pick out any one man for commendation. They all behaved admirably under the most trying circumstance and upheld the highest traditions of the service." In one case the commanding officer reported the fact that he had been depth-charged for several hours by enemy patrols. His report simply stated the bald fact. The Admiralty asked for a report on how the crew had behaved under the trying circumstances and received this as a reply: "The crew, seeing their officers took the incident simply as one which could reasonably be expected when patrolling in enemy waters, settled themselves down again to read or resume their interrupted game of cards."

When Lieutenant Holbrook, V. C., returned from the Dardanelles he was given command of a new mine-laying submarine, *E-41*. It was said that the Admiralty offered to decorate each and every man who did eight mine-laying trips into the Bight of Heligoland. When this order was promulgated one man remarked: "God! ain't they generous? I don't think. The odds are 100 to 1 they'll never have to decorate a single crew." The man was not very far off either.

Our mine-laying submarines did wonderful work and took extraordinary risks, but I am afraid their efforts were poorly rewarded in as much as they failed to inflict nearly the damage on enemy ships that the enemy mine-laying boats inflicted on us.

It was generally conceded in the service that our mines were not nearly so effective as those of the enemy, while our depth charges were far more deadly.

Our mine-laying submarines laid their nests of eggs like a female bass and then the other boats

hovered in the vicinity like a male bass watching
the nest and hoping something belonging to the
enemy would steam into the middle of it.

Time and again they saw enemy ships steam into
the area just mined but they watched for results
in vain. The H. M. S. *Vernon* was our mining-
depot ship. One of our boats while patrolling submerged hit a mine. The deadly engine of destruction hit on the port bow and the clanging sound
vibrated through the boat like a church bell tolling
the passing of some soul. The crew all stood or sat
motionless where they were. There was nothing
they could do. The mine bounced off and swung
in again and crashed against the side farther aft.
Still the men waited. They held their breath. They
felt that the least movement or sound they might
make would cause the thing to explode. Seconds
which seemed like eternities passed and the deadly
C-L-A-N-G reëchoed through the boat again. As it
hit for the third time and failed to explode one of
the men said quite unconcernedly, "Good old *Vernon,* another bloody dud!"

The tension in the boat snapped. Everyone burst
out laughing. They couldn't help it.

I always noticed that the natural reaction from
sudden danger and suspense was to laugh, as the
crew of that E-boat laughed while the mine went
clanging and rolling along the boat's side and
finally washed clear of the stern. When this story
was told in official circles the man was decorated.

The incident which proved that Holbrook's exploit in *B-11*, while in the Dardanelles, was no mere flash in the pan occurred while I was at Harwich.

He set out with a load of mines which had to be laid in the Bight. He took his boat right into one of the enemy channels close to one of their bases. When he arrived off the position chosen to lay the mine field he found a flotilla of mine sweepers at work. He watched them closely through his periscope and then followed them in, and mined the channel on his way out again. As she finished her task, *E-41* sighted a German merchant ship being escorted by several patrol craft. Holbrook manœuvred into position and fired a torpedo which sank the ship. The patrol craft promptly chased him. Showing his periscope periodically so that the vessels chasing him would not lose his trail, he steered to the mines he had just laid, hoping to be able to test their effectiveness. When he had coaxed the enemy vessels into the vicinity he dived deep to avoid them himself and proceeded to creep through the field, keeping close to the sea bed. Having done this, he had the disappointment of seeing the patrol vessels turn back just as they were headed straight into the trap he had so ingeniously made.

There is also the story of the man who acted as officer's servant in a boat which was depth-charged just at breakfast time. He had carefully prepared

breakfast and made some coffee. The depth charge
upset the whole works and as the man gathered up
the débris he plaintively remarked to the captain,
"The blighters upset your coffee, sir, but I'll make
another cup."

Another meal was interrupted just as it finished.
The coffee was being served. The officer on watch
sighted an enemy submarine. The attack was a
long-drawn-out affair because the other boat kept
changing course. After about an hour's manœu-
vrying, trying to get into a position for a sure shot,
the captain of the submarine gave the order:
"Stand by your bow tubes. We're going to fire in
three minutes." Hearing a definite time set, the signal rating, who acted as officer's steward, inquired,
"Will you have your coffee now or later, sir?" I
regret to record that the officer in question, perhaps owing to the strain of one of the most drawn-
out attacks on record, told his man to get to hell
out of his way. Then he ordered "Raise periscope,"
gave it the little twist which allowed for the correct deflection, as a man must do when shooting
at a moving target, and gave the command: "Fire."
Before the torpedo hit, the signal rating was at his
elbow again. "Here's your coffee, sir."

And there was the cockney who intended to buy
a motor bike if he ever was lucky enough to win
any blood money. The opportunity came one day.
A three-funnelled cruiser was attacked but the
torpedo missed. From the moment the torpedo left

the tube the cockney began to count one-two-three, etc. He knew that the torpedo should reach its objective in forty-five seconds. When he had counted fifty without the shock of the explosion being felt he was heard to remark: "Hum! There goes my ruddy motor bike!"

But it is almost impossible to give any idea of the sang-froid of the men. Take the G-boat which got entangled in the trawl of a fishing vessel off Horn's Reef. The trawler had been sighted at a distance. A decoy vessel had been reported as operating in the vicinity. The G-boat dashed off to inspect her at close quarters. She got to within a few hundred yards and then noticed that what had been taken for a gun mounted on the for'ard deck was in reality a spar. The submarine proceeded to inspect the trawler from the other side to make sure she was an innocent craft. In diving to go under her the G-boat became entangled in some form of obstruction. The crew naturally thought that they had fallen victim to a well-prepared trap. Nothing they could do while submerged would break them clear. They plunged, dived, dashed ahead, and then reversed the motors and went full speed astern, but all to no avail. The captain of the submarine decided to come to the surface and fight with his gun. Ammunition was placed under the for'ard hatch; the crew stood ready to man the gun the moment the hatch opened. Men were detailed to pass up ammunition, and two others were detailed to take axes and cut adrift the wires which entangled them.

The tanks were blown. The boat bobbed to the surface. Hatches were thrown open. The gun crew closed up, and the two men detailed for the job jumped to their task of cutting the wires by which the boat was held.

Reporting the incident afterward, said the commanding officer: "Notwithstanding the fact that we were all convinced that we were dealing with an enemy decoy ship, the men detailed to cut the wires set about their task as soon as they reached the deck and never once raised their backs or turned their heads until the job was finished."

As it turned out, they were foul of an innocent trawler's gear, but men have to be well trained and have courage to act as they did when expecting a salvo of shells to hit them every moment.

(2)

I know of no deed ashore or afloat performed during the war which can compare with that of Stoker Petty Officer William Brown, one of the crew of a submarine which was accidentally sunk off Harwich while engaged in torpedo practice with another submarine for the target.

To exercise officers in making attacks under conditions as near as possible to those they would experience while patrolling enemy waters, a submarine would be detailed to act as target while others took turns attacking her.

Two boats would go to sea and one would submerge. The other would proceed until it was well out of sight and then return on the surface, just as an enemy boat would do when nearing her base. It was wonderful practice and both officers and men were always keen to indulge in it. On the day in question the officer commanding the attacking, or submerged, submarine sighted his quarry a long way off. He estimated the target's course and speed, then as the sea was calm lowered his periscope and headed his boat on a course to intercept her.

This game was played very keenly. The lookouts on the target knew they were being attacked and they were alert, watching for the first sight of the attacking boat's periscope. If they succeeded in seeing it, all they had to do was put the helm hard over and defeat the other's efforts. Naturally, the less the attacking submarine used her periscope the better chance she had of hitting the target. The torpedoes used were fitted with a special collapsible head which mushroomed when it struck and in that manner absorbed the shock which might otherwise have damaged the delicate mechanism of the torpedo.

On this occasion the attacking officer delayed too long before raising his periscope. When he did, it broke surface less than fifty yards ahead of the target. A collision was unavoidable and the boat

on the surface crashed into the conning tower of
the one submerged.

The submerged boat had her conning tower
badly damaged, but this in no way affected her sea-
worthiness. The target submarine was, however,
badly holed below the water line for'ard, and began to fill and sink. The captain of the target submarine ordered all hands on deck. Petty Officer
Brown and two other men didn't receive the order
and went down with the boat. The conning-tower
hatch was open when the boat sank.

Could a more terrifying experience be imagined? Yet Petty Officer Brown lived to tell the
story of what happened in the bowels of that submarine, sixty-five feet below the surface of the
North Sea.

He made himself out to be no hero. He told a
plain, straightforward story of what happened and
what he did to cope with the situation, and it is
only by taking note of the wealth of detail with
which he told of every phase of the astounding
event that one can begin to realize with what extraordinary courage and coolness he mastered a
situation with which only one man in a million
would have even tried to cope. Most men would
have surrendered to the inevitable and died. Not
so Petty Officer Brown.

When the boat hit the bottom the other two
men, one a stoker, the other an engine-room artificer, found themselves in a pocket of air. They

were standing in the midship compartment not far from the conning tower hatch. They waited for a second or two, sizing up the situation, and then, realizing that the boat was full of water and that the faint gleam of light they saw ahead was probably from the conning tower hatch they took a deep breath and dived in the direction of the light. They made the conning tower ladder, saw light above them, pulled themselves upward and clear of the hatch, and reached the surface to the intense amazement of the crews of the vessels which had been summoned to the spot the moment the accident was known.

Petty Officer Brown was the only one missing. In the hope that he might have succeeded in shutting himself inside one of the compartments which had remained watertight, they sent frantic signals asking for salvage equipment and divers. Brown was a man worthy of any effort. The stoker and the engine-room artificer, who owed their lives to their wonderful presence of mind, reported having seen Brown as the boat was sinking. The E. R. A. had asked him if all men were out of the engine room. Brown deliberately walked from under the open conning tower hatch and safety, replying, "I will go and see." He walked through the midship compartment and into the engine room. He met the stoker and told him: "Keep your head. The boat has sunk. Put on a life belt, and take your turn at the conning tower hatch."

Brown's own story was one of direct simplicity:
"Something was heard to come in contact with the
bottom of the boat for'ard. It hit twice in quick
succession. Then the engine-room telegraph rang:
'Out clutches.' I took out the port clutch and closed
the muffler valve, then I heard the report that the
boat was making water. I proceeded for'ard to
ascertain the position of the leak, and came to the
conclusion she was holed low down. My first im-
pulse was to close the lower conning-tower hatch.
At this point the chief engine-room artificer asked
me if all hands were out of the engine room. I replied that I would go and find out. On going aft
I met one man coming for'ard. I ordered him to
put his life belt on, keep his head, and go to the
conning-tower hatch and wait his turn. Finding
there was nobody else aft, I came for'ard and put
on a life belt and closed the valve on the air trunk
through the engine-room bulkhead. Then I noticed
the water begin to come down the conning-tower
hatch, and the boat took a dip by the bows."

For the reader's benefit, I might say that probably a minute and a half or two minutes elapsed
from the time the boats were in collision until the
water began to pour down the hatch which had
been left open to allow everyone to get out. But
Brown had not received the order to leave and it is
quite evident he went about his ordinary routine
duties up to this point. To continue Brown's report: "I then went aft and shouted to the hands

for'ard to come to the engine room. There was no response. The midship compartment was in darkness and partly flooded. Chlorine gas began to come through. I closed the engine-room door and began to unscrew the clips of the torpedo hatch above me. At this juncture the engine room was in complete darkness, with the exception of the port pilot lamp which was evidently burning through 'earth.' The water was slowly rising in the engine room through the voice pipes which I had left open to relieve the pressure on the bulkhead door.

"I proceeded to disconnect the torpedo hatch from its gearing, which meant the removal of two split pins and two pins from the links. Before the foremost one could be moved I had to unship the strong-back and wait for sufficient pressure in the boat to ease the hatch off the strong-back."

The outside pressure was such that the hatch was jammed down tight and could not have been opened by human strength. The only thing Brown could do was wait until the water flooding into the engine-room compartment through the voice pipes rose to a sufficient depth to equalize the pressure in the compartment with that outside the hull. To get a true impression of what the man had to contend with, it must be remembered that he was working practically in darkness, in electrically charged water up to his middle, and was choking with the fumes of chlorine gas which trickled in through the voice pipes leading from the control

room. The hatch he was trying to open was a heavy
one. It was situated over his head and in an awkward position to work at. Brown's knowledge of
the boat and its contents was such that he could
grope about among that maze of machinery in the
dark with the deftness and sureness of a blind man
in his own room at home.

"The heat at this time was excessive, therefore,
I rested awhile and considered the best way of
flooding the engine room. I eventually decided that
the best way would be to flood it through the stern
tube or the weed trap of the circulating system, or
by dropping the exhaust and induction valves and
opening the muffler valve. I tried the stern tube
first, but I could open neither the stern cap nor the
rear door. Then I came for'ard again. While passing the switchboards I received several shocks. I
tried to open the weed trap of the circulating inlet
but it was in an awkward position, and as the water
was coming over the top of me I could not ease
back the butterfly nuts. So I proceeded for'ard
again and opened the muffler valve, also the test
cocks on the group-exhaust valves. I tried them and
found the water coming in. I then climbed on top
of the engines underneath the torpedo hatch and
unshipped the strong-back, drawing the pin out of
the link with a spanner I had with me. In order to
flood the boat completely, I opened the scuttle in
the engine-room bulkhead."

He did this to increase the pressure in the engine

room to a sufficient extent to enable him to open the hatch wide and be forced through it to the surface.

"Chlorine gas came in as well as water. I tried three times to lift the hatch but each time could open it only halfway, and each time air rushed out through it and the hatch fell down. I clipped the hatch again and had to dive down to fetch the clip bolts; then as the pressure increased again I knocked off the clip bolts. The hatch flew open, but not enough to let me out. I managed to lift it sufficiently to clear my hand and let it down again. I then decided to flood the boat rapidly through the dead-light, till the water came up level with the hatch coaming. I was then able to raise the hatch and come to the surface."

It was an hour and a half from the time the submarine sank until the crew of the destroyer which was marking the spot suddenly saw a man come bobbing, like a cork, to the surface. He had on an air belt and had a badly crushed hand. He appeared all in, but he wasn't. As soon as he was fished out of the water he started to give detailed information to the officers in charge of the salvage operation. He told them where he thought the damage was, what valves were open and closed, which of the bulkhead doors were closed, and a wealth of technical information which the lay reader would not understand but which was of the utmost value to those who had to raise the boat.

CHAPTER SIXTEEN

A SENSE of humour went a long way toward making life pleasant aboard submarines. Lieutenant Commander Kellett, who commanded Submarine *S-1,* had a real sense of humour and the patience of Job. The S-class boats were misfits in every way. According to officers who served in them, they were everything a submarine ought not to be. They were most unreliable, and after the first few were tested out on active service the construction of them was discontinued.

Imagine being on patrol nine miles north of Heligoland in command of a boat in which you had no confidence. That was the position in which Lieutenant Kellett found himself on June 21, 1915. To make matters worse, he had to stay submerged and to keep out of the way of one zeppelin, one seaplane, and nineteen armed trawlers which were busy sweeping the patrol position, and all this on the first day. Then, to liven things up, a destroyer was sighted. Kellett attacked and fired a torpedo but without securing a hit. That night *S-1's* port engine broke down completely while she was on the surface recharging her batteries.

Next day, still carrying on, Kellett sighted another zeppelin and a parseval. The crew worked all day to repair the damaged engines and continued the diving patrol on the motors.

To fill the cup of sorrow to the brim, the starboard engines broke down on the 23d. The crew were forced to stay under because zeppelins were in sight all day and, sweating and swearing, they worked another day submerged trying to repair the engines. Only those who have tried to work inside a submerged submarine can realize just what the task is like. I never experienced any very bad effects from a diving patrol of eighteen hours unless I had to move around a lot toward the end of the diving period. Then breathing was difficult and heavy, and lethargy stole over me and a cross-headache invariably developed.

The damaged engines refused to respond to the efforts of the crew. The 24th of June found *S-1* with her batteries run down and no means of recharging them. She was in enemy waters, surrounded by enemy aircraft and patrols, and the crew would have been perfectly justified had they come up and surrendered. They might have done so if it hadn't been for Kellett's sense of humour. There came a time when the ocean was calm and unbroken except for one solitary trawler in sight. With the last of his precious juice, Kellett drove *S-1* over in her direction. He came to the surface close on her beam and, manning his gun, demanded her surrender. Not knowing the sad plight the British submarine was in, the German crew complied with the command without firing a shot.

Lieutenant Kennedy, Kellett's first lieutenant, took five men and boarded the trawler. A towline was passed and the trawler headed for Yarmouth. *S-1* dragged along at the end of the tow and kept the other vessel's crew under control with the threat of the forward gun.

But Kellett's luck was dead out. He must have sailed on a Friday, for on the 25th the German trawler's engines broke down. The submarine laid alongside and her crew set to work and repaired the engines. They had to refit the H. P. piston, crossheads, and crankhead bearings. After they had finished, the best speed they could get out of the old ruin was four knots, and they were not as yet clear of the Bight. On the 26th the trawler's L. P. cylinder went on the blink and it was necessary to stop again. The crew cursed and worked some more with the result that they got under way again and actually arrived in Yarmouth unassisted, in tow of their prize, on the 27th of June.

To a Canadian, Lieutenant Commander B. L. Johnson, R. N. R., must go the credit for one of the finest feats performed in the annals of submarines. The extraordinary thing is that this officer was not a highly trained submarine officer with years of peace-time training. He was in the British Merchant Service before the war and was appointed to bring *H-8* over from Halifax. She was one of the boats constructed on that side of the Atlantic. *H-8* made her way across the Atlantic Ocean long before the world went mad about the feat performed by the *Deutschland*. Lieutenant Johnson was "submarine-minded." He loved them. He trained a crew consisting of nearly all reserve ratings like himself until they were the equal of any crew in the service. They were nearly all Canadian or Scotch. So well did this crew perform when they arrived at Harwich with their boat that Lieutenant Johnson was allowed to retain his command and take her out on active service. He was the first officer of the Royal Naval Reserve to command a submarine. Several more were given this honour before the war ended. With less than four years' experience, they proved themselves qualified and the confidence placed in them was never regretted. Many more reserve officers were serving as first lieutenants of submarines when hostilities ended. They knew nothing of engines and ma-

chinery when the war broke out. They joined submarines as navigating officers, and for watch-
keeping duties, but quickly mastered the most
complicated work in the service. They were used to
supply the need for experienced officers due to the
intensive building programme and the vacancies
which occurred through the wastage of war.

Submarine *H-8* was patrolling off Ameland Gat
on March 22, 1916, when those inside of her heard
a slight scraping noise forward. They were down
at sixty feet at the time and hardly had they heard
the weird sound than the boat rocked under the
influence of a terrific explosion. The submarine
sank by the bows and hit bottom at an angle of between 25 and 30 degrees in eighty-five feet of
water. She had struck a mine, and when it exploded against the starboard forward hydroplane
both forward hydroplanes were blown off, the bow
caps protecting the torpedo tubes torn off, the torpedo tubes themselves wrecked, and the hull was
badly damaged. Number 1 tank was ripped open
to the sea.

If it were not for the fact that her crew returned
to Harwich and brought their crippled boat back
with them, this story would never have been written. Johnson's report of the affair was, as might
be expected, exceedingly brief:

"The forward bulkhead, although leaking, happened to hold. The watertight doors were closed.
The motors were put full astern and Numbers 2

and 3 ballast tanks were blown. Number 1 tank was found to be open to the sea. The submarine then came to the surface. After blowing some fuel and making some temporary repairs, course was shaped for Terschelling and then Harwich."

The flotilla captain of the *Maidstone* wrote, reporting on the matter: "The captain [Johnson] reports that although it appeared obvious to all that the boat was lost, the officers and entire crew proceeded to their stations without any sign of excitement, and all orders were carried out promptly and correctly. I would submit that such conduct, in the face of apparent certain death is an example of which the whole service may be proud."

(2)

Although the story has been told before, and told by more able writers than I, I feel some mention should be made of the part *C-3* took in the raid that the British Fleet made on Zeebrugge. Lieutenant Howell-Price, the officer I relieved in Submarine *G-6* when I first joined the service, was the one chosen to accompany Lieutenant R. D. Sandford and his small but select crew who were detailed to blow up the mole.

Great secrecy was maintained previous to the attack, for surprise was an element necessary to the success of the operation. After Price left *G-6* he went down to Fort Blockhouse for a course, and after he had completed his course he was appointed

to *C-3* as her first lieutenant. She was an old, old
boat, and long past the retiring age. Howell-Price
was not very pleased with his appointment at first,
but then he had no idea of the special duty his boat
had been selected to perform. He had been engaged
for some time and arrangements were made for his
marriage. I heard that a gentle hint reached him
that it would perhaps be better if he put his wedding off for a little while longer. Without giving
away the real reason for the delay, excuses were
made and the wedding postponed.

Then came the day when ships manned by crews
who had been hand-picked from every ship in the
navy set out to storm the mole and blockade the
harbour of Zeebrugge. The navy had not been
nearly as active as the men who manned the ships
would have liked it to be. To give them a chance
to distinguish themselves at least once, it was arranged that those who took part in the raid on Zeebrugge should be picked from volunteers from
every ship. First of all, each ship was detailed a
given number of officers, petty officers, and men.
Then volunteers were asked for, and from those who
volunteered "for special duty" the final selections
were made. To those selected was entrusted the
honour of their ships. According to their personal
conduct the courage of the navy was to be judged.
That they upheld the honour of the navy, I think
the whole world is agreed.

So it was that *C-3* and her crew of two officers

and seven men, received the honour of upholding
the record of the Trade. Their task was to approach as near as possible to the viaduct which
separated the mole from the shore and then, after
heading the old submarine for the trellis work, to
fire the fuse and escape by means of a small motorboat they towed astern. The steering gear in *C-3*
had been fixed so that she would steer herself for the last few hundred yards of her final
journey before she died to the noise of her own
thunder.

But these men upon whose shoulders rested so
much responsibility refused to trust to any mechanical device. As they made their way across to
the Flanders coast they decided they would take
the boat right under the viaduct before they blew
her up.

Perhaps the sheer audacity of their plan made
for its success. Unless the German troops who lined
the top of the mole thought the crew of *C-3* was
lost or had gone crazy, it is hard to understand why
they were allowed to proceed until they had actually jammed the hull of the obsolete old submarine
hard and fast between the pilings which carried
the viaduct from the mole to the shore. The fact re-
mains that they did. The enemy seems to have
remained inactive until the crew of *C-3* began to
scramble into their small boat. Then the Germans
came to life with a vengeance. Hundreds of German troops opened fire with machine guns and

rifles. To make matters worse, the propeller of the motorboat was lost just as *C-3's* crew was about to push off from the submarine. Inside the boat the lighted fuse spluttered toward tons of high explosive. Seconds only remained for escape. Two men grabbed the two small paddles which were in the boat and started to pull for all they were worth.

Bullets cut through the planking of their frail craft and splashed into the water all around them. As one man sank to the bottom of the boat, pierced with a bullet, another took the oars and kept pulling. In this way they were nearly two hundred yards from *C-3* when, with a flash and a roar, she blew up, completely demolishing the viaduct and sending some hundreds of enemy troops to their death.

Sandford said afterward: "I was not able to enjoy seeing the full spectacle of the explosion because, just as it occurred, I was wounded." So was every other man in the boat except Howell-Price. He, in some miraculous way, escaped harm. While men and débris fell splashing into the water all around them and Price was trying to hold his own with the small oars against the strong tide, a steam pinnace commanded by Lieutenant Commander Sandford, the submarine commander's older brother, drew alongside and pulled them up.

Although all the men except Price were wounded and most of them seriously, they kept on asking like rooters after a football match, "Have

we won. . . . Have we won?" On the *Vindictive* the
men stopped fighting to give three rousing cheers
when the explosion announced the success of the
submarine's attack on the viaduct. Such was the
spirit of Zeebrugge carried out on St. George's
Day, 1918. And sad it is to relate that, after recovering from his wounds and receiving the Victoria
Cross for his deeds, Lieutenant Sandford fell victim to pneumonia and died before the armistice
was signed. Lieutenant Howell-Price was married
within a few hours after the boat put ashore. He
was given command of another C-boat and remained in the service until the end of the war.

(3)

Contrary to general belief, accidents were very
rare in British submarines during the war. When
they did occur, and boats sank as the result of them,
the conduct of the officers and men was an inspiration to the rest of those who served in the underseas
branch of the service.

C-12 sank in the Humber. She was making her
way down river when the main motors went wrong.
Before the anchors could be dropped she was
swung by the strong ebb tide and smashed against
the bows of some destroyers which were moored at
the eastern jetty, at Immingham. She was badly
holed and began to sink.

Most of the crew, including the first lieutenant,
were below at the time, but the officer in command,

Lieutenant Manley, was on the conning tower. He ordered all hands to come up on deck. Lieutenant Sullivan sent everyone up in compliance with the captain's orders but remained below himself, closing watertight doors and trying to ascertain the full extent of damage.

As the last man scrambled out on deck the captain jumped below and went to assist his first lieutenant. He closed the lid of the hatch after him as he saw the boat was actually sinking. The boat hit the bottom as he finished descending the ladder into the control room.

An examination showed that nothing could be done without the assistance of a salvage vessel. Water had reached the batteries and chlorine gas was filling the control room. The two officers reëntered the conning tower and, closing the lower hatch, flooded the conning tower itself; then, when the pressure inside and out was equal, they opened the upper hatch and calmly swam to the surface where they reported that nothing could be done without a salvage plant to lift the boat.

It is only men who are "submarine-minded" who can act like that. It is exactly the same with men and women who wish to fly. To make a success they must be "air-minded." No amount of technical training can supply this quality if it is not there naturally. The man who is "submarine-minded" invariably feels safer down below than on the surface.

Lieutenant Lowther, R. N. R., who served with me in submarine *R-12,* was responsible for saving his boat after she had been damaged in the Firth of Forth. The whole flotilla of K-class submarines became entangled in the darkness with the battle-cruiser squadron. Two of them were sunk and others damaged. The accident happened during the early part of 1918. The fleet was putting to sea for a stunt. The K-class submarines were the first to sail. They were to speed ahead of the other ships and take up their battle stations at daylight.

The night was dark and rainy. Visibility was very low. One of the submarines developed engine trouble and reported the fact to her senior officer. I served in Submarine *K-12* in 1918 and I can assure the reader that it was no easy matter to keep station when weather conditions were bad and the engines behaving like a man with asthma. Owing to the trouble with her engines, this particular K-boat found it impossible to keep station at all. First she was charging into the stern of the boat next ahead, and then falling back to be nearly rammed in turn by the next astern. The senior officer ordered her to return to port. The signal was sent by Morse lamp and it was read by all submarines and interpreted to be a general signal for all to return to port. The boats turned sixteen points and within a few minutes the light cruisers, dashing to sea at full speed, were crashing through their lines. Two submarines were sunk and two others damaged. Lieutenant Lowther saved his boat by staying below and shutting all watertight doors before he attempted to get on deck himself.

K-boats never did have an opportunity to distinguish themselves in action with the enemy, or to show if the purpose for which they were constructed was feasible. They were nothing more nor less than modern destroyers capable of submerging. They could fight with their 4.1-inch guns when on the surface, and dive to deliver their torpedo attack. They had ten 21-inch torpedo tubes and were capable of steaming at twenty-five knots on the surface and a little better than ten knots submerged. They required four minutes to dive, and had to be very carefully handled, owing to their great length. They were 297 feet long and had more than two thousand tons displacement. It can be readily seen that if they dived or rose at a steep angle they would be bumping the bottom in many sections of the North Sea.

It was another accident to a K-boat, *K-13,* which robbed the service of one of its most promising and gallant officers, Lieutenant Commander Goodhart, D. S. O. The reader already knows the type of man he was from his operations in the Baltic. It will be easy to understand then how when *K-13* met with her accident and lay helpless on the bottom of the Gair Loch with her crew imprisoned inside of her, Goodhart, although only a passenger on her at the time, sacrificed his own life so that they might be saved.

After his return from the Baltic he was appointed to command one of the new K-class submarines. While his boat was completing he went out on *K-13*—that number which proved so unlucky to all classes except the G-class. Commander Herbert was the boat's commander and Goodhart went along to watch her trials. *K-13* dived, and owing to some circumstances which have never been explained, she dived with her ventilators open. The engine room and boiler room flooded and she sank to the bottom in seventy feet of water. All the men in the two compartments which flooded were drowned.

When she came to rest on the bottom of the Gair Loch those surviving did not know that an E-class submarine which was in the vicinity had seen her go down and realized that she was in difficulties.

But those inside did not know help was at hand. They had done everything possible to get the boat to the surface and failed. Goodhart was a passenger. He told Commander Herbert that it was Herbert's place as captain of the boat to stay with his men and that he would try to reach the surface and communicate their predicament to the outside world.

Goodhart outlined his plans. "Let me go into the conning tower and close the lower lid. Then flood the lower conning tower until the pressure inside is equal to that outside the boat. When I give you the signal, put compressed air into the lower conning tower and it will help me to the surface. If any boat is in the vicinity I will tell it what has happened." . . . He did not say that if no boat was in the vicinity he was doomed. He knew the risk he ran from the great pressure. He knew that if he reached the surface and was picked up he would probably die, even if he lived long enough to give his message.

Commander Herbert agreed to Goodhart's taking this desperate chance. He accompanied Goodhart into the conning tower, to see if he got out all right. The compartment was flooded. The water rose until it reached their necks. Then they felt the hiss of compressed air rushing into the compartment in which they stood. They clasped hands. "Good luck, Goodhart," was the last words Herbert spoke to him. Goodhart opened the top lid and the air forced him through the opening like a shot out of a gun. He struck his head against some projection and was killed. But his sacrifice was not to be in vain for Herbert, who stood ready to close the hatch the moment he was clear, found himself pushed forcibly upward. He couldn't help himself. He went upward and upward, passed safely through the upper lid, cleared all the projections, and was carried to the surface in a bubble of air. "I felt no discomfort and was able to breathe the whole way," he told the astonished salvage crew who fished him out of the water.

With the valuable information he was able to give those in charge of the operations, tubes were attached to the ammunition hoist of the sunken K-boat and the men inside of her were given air and food until it was possible to attach wires to the boat and raise one end out of the water. This enabled the crew to escape through one of the hatches. And Fate was kind to them, for the very moment the last man was out the wires parted and *K-13* sank once more to the bottom of the Gair Loch.

It has often been a subject of speculation what the experiences are of men who are entombed inside a submarine. It was Wednesday afternoon before the men of *K-13* were rescued. They had been imprisoned for two days. They reported that they just grew tired and went into a sort of semi-coma. They didn't worry about being rescued, but sank into a state of calm indifference. Death inside a submarine is not so horrible as some might suppose if only the men do not become panic-stricken; if panic breaks out nothing can be more terrible.

(4)

As submarines had been the first to put to sea in 1914, so were they the last to be withdrawn in 1918. On Armistice Day I was on patrol in the new submarine *R-12*. We were proceeding to a

position off the northwest coast of Ireland to way-
lay a German submarine flotilla reported homeward bound from the Mediterranean. On the
morning of November 11th we were proceeding as
requisite on the surface, Lieutenant Barry and I
leaning with our arms over the periscope standard
and facing in opposite directions. Suddenly the
first lieutenant struggled through the hatch and
handed Barry a signal. I glanced at Barry's face
and seeing the expression on it threw caution to the
winds while I read the signal he handed to me:
"Armistice will be signed 11 A. M. Cease hostilities
unless attacked."

I would be foolish to try to explain my feelings.
I can tell, however, what we did. The first thing
was to send a signal asking if we might return from
patrol. The reply we got was very curt and plain.
"Remain on patrol until ordered to return." That
was that. The war was over but there was still a
navy—a disciplined navy.

Of that navy, the submarine service was credited
with sinking during the period of hostilities 54
enemy warships and 274 transports and supply
ships, or ships engaged in contraband trade. These
numbers do not include those ships of the enemy
forces which were torpedoed by our boats which
succeeded in reaching port. They do include, however, the nineteen enemy U-boats which fell prey
to the marksmanship of our submarine commanders. Admiral S. S. Hall, in an order issued

after the armistice, gave the submarine service, which he commanded, credit for sinking more enemy submarines and for doing more to counter the enemy's illegal war upon commerce than any other single factor.

It was not alone in the number of U-boats actually sunk that the value of our submarines against the U-boat can be measured. There was the moral effect to be considered. Next to patrolling in the known presence of mine fields which have to be negotiated but cannot be seen, I know of nothing worse on the nerves than patrolling on the surface in a locality in which other submarines may be patrolling submerged. If it should so happen that on one or two occasions you have just been able to avoid sudden death by the quick action of the helm, the effect is even more pronounced. This feeling of insecurity undoubtedly kept enemy submarines underneath the surface a great deal more than would have been the case if our submarines had not been hunting them, and if they had not been kept under they would have been able to sink far more of our merchant ships than they did.

For instance, what must the moral effect have been on the men of the U-boat service when *E-45's* feat became known to them? Lieutenant Commander G. R. S. Watkins sighted flashes on the horizon at dawn one October morning. He was on the surface at the time and altered course to investigate. He found a U-boat shelling a merchant ship.

He dived before the U-boat sighted him. The merchant ship was a neutral and unarmed. The U-boat had shelled her beneath the water line and was sitting there waiting to see her sink. *E-45* was manœuvred to within four hundred yards of the enemy U-boat and a well-aimed torpedo sent her to the bottom just as the Dutch ship took her final plunge.

Many Germans rescued by our submarines said they feared the uncertainty of attack from our boats far more than they did the certainty of attack from destroyers they knew had sighted them.

Nineteen was a very fair bag, considering the conditions our boats were forced to operate under and the smallness of the target. It must be admitted that torpedoes, that is eighteen-inch torpedoes, did not seem to have sufficient power to deal a death blow to a modern battleship. Our submarine commanders were doomed to many disappointments on this account. After accepting all the risks involved in attacking a well-protected fleet, Lieutenant Commander Turner in *E-23* hit but failed to sink the 18,000-ton battleship *Westfalen*. More annoying still, Commander Laurence on November 5, 1916, in *J-1* achieved the brilliant coup of torpedoing two enemy dreadnoughts, the *Grosser Kurfürst* and the *Kronprinz*. Both were battleships of the very latest type. They were both hard hit and both succeeded in getting back to port. I remember Laurence once saying: "How I wish I had fired both torpedoes at the one ship and made sure

of her . . . but I thought I could bag them both."
And it was not that the German battleships were
any more lucky or better built than our own. During the Battle of Jutland, H. M. S. *Marlborough*
was hit by a torpedo and continued in action hardly
inconvenienced at all. Considering the lack of targets our submarines had, their successes against
the armed ships of the enemy seem to have been beyond comparison with what U-boats did to our
surface armed ships, which were at sea most of
the time.

To achieve these successes we lost sixty-one submarines, a far different number from the total the
navy boasted at the outbreak of hostilities. One
man out of every three in the Trade paid with his
life. Of these sixty-one boats, twenty sailed to the
port of missing ships. They left for their patrol
positions and were never heard of again. Not even
a careful check after the war of the enemy records
threw any light on their fate. They probably struck
mines. Seven of our boats were blown up in the
Baltic without loss of life, to prevent their capture
by the enemy after the Russians signed a separate
peace with the Central Powers. *C-3* was also destroyed by her own crew. Five of our boats were
sunk by the torpedoes or gunfire of enemy submarines. Four more were known to have been sunk
by mines off our own coast. Three were lost
attempting to force their way into the Sea of Marmora, and one sank as the result of shell fire from

Turkish ships. Two were sunk by bombs dropped
by aircraft. One, a D-class submarine, fell victim
to the bombs of a French airship, another was sunk
alongside her mooring place in port during an
air raid. Seven were sunk as the results of collision
with boats of our own fleet. Three others were sunk
in error when mistaken for enemy submarines.
Three were wrecked on neutral coasts, one on our
own coast, and one in the Baltic. One sank in harbour, one while doing her trials, and one was sunk
by gunfire of enemy ships after sinking a destroyer
in the Bight. It will be seen that our losses were
due to vastly different causes than those which sent
to the bottom 284 enemy submarines.

It will be seen that twenty-five of our boats were
lost as the results of other than enemy action,
twenty-four can be credited to enemy mines, and
twelve to other enemy action. It is to the lasting
credit of the officers of the Royal Naval Reserve
that only four boats were lost as the result of errors
in navigation. Considering the conditions, this is a
truly remarkable record. None of our boats surrendered. We, on the other hand, did capture some
of the enemy submarines, most notably *UC-5*, one
of their mine-laying submarines, which was afterward exhibited in London.

When the war ended there were less than a
dozen enemy submarines at sea. Many of their
boats were tied up for want of trained crews to
man them. We, on the other hand, had no shortage

of volunteers during the whole period of the war.
The number and the type of men who volunteered
allowed those in charge to pick the very best and
most suitable men for the work.

Nor can we forget the heroic fortitude of the
women of the British Submarine Service. I can
imagine nothing more torturing to nerves than the
part they played. Soon after the depots were
properly organized the married officers and men
were encouraged to have their wives live near the
depots. They were there with a cheerful smile and
sympathetic understanding which did a lot to overcome frayed nerves and make up for weeks of cold
discomfort. Their share in the war was, in my
opinion, as trying and as dangerous as that played
by any combatant. They were living in areas constantly being raided by enemy air fleets. They had
the long weary waits from the time their menfolk
left on patrol until they returned, weeks when they
could do nothing but hope and pray. I know of
nothing sadder than to see a little group gathering
one by one on the end of the jetty or the end of the
wharf gazing out to the eastward when one of the
boats was overdue. The women would stand there
for hours, outwardly calm, dried-eyed, but suffering the agony of doubt and uncertainty, hoping
against hope that some accident or some defective
machinery had caused the delay, but feeling in
their hearts that their boat had sailed to the port of
missing ships.

(5)

The war is a thing of the past, its horrors and its lessons already dimmed by time. Of those horrors, no weapon, save possibly gas, so preyed on the imagination of the world as did the submarine. Some countries wish to retain its use; others are willing to abandon it. What of its future?

If the story of the German undersea raiders shows clearly the possibilities of the submarine, this story of the British Trade should convey just as clearly its limitations. Both records merge to emphasize one fact, and that possibly the most important of all in determining the future use of the weapon, particularly in those countries which steadfastly refuse to scrap it.

To be successful, submarines must be manned by crews of volunteers of the right type—men who know the risks they run and accept them impassionately. One British submarine sank and was not raised for three weeks. When she was brought to the surface her crew were all found dead at their posts. Most of them had written a final message to their friends and relatives. The letters were simple farewells; there were no heroics, no hysterics. They told what had been done to save the boat, and failing in that how they had tried to save themselves. Their efforts proving abortive, they resigned themselves to death. They died where, under ordinary conditions, they had slept.

These are the type of men on whom the success of the submarine depends. It may be possible to produce submarines by mass production which will more than make up for the wastage of war, but with anti-submarine methods as effective as they were at the end of the war, I doubt very much that crews could be found and, if found, be trained to man them properly. No matter what experts may say, no matter what figures may prove, no matter what modern science may invent, this fact is certain: the value of submarines as engines of war will always be limited by the skill and courage of the crews that man them.

THE END

INDEX

INDEX

306 INDEX

THE CURSE OF THE BALTIC

The most persistent enemy of submarine warfare
in northern waters, where England achieved some
spectacular victories, was ice. This is a photograph of E. G. Max Horton's boat.

www.ingramcontent.com/pod-product-compliance
Lightning Source LLC
Chambersburg PA
CBHW030911090426
42737CB00007B/156